Amazing Animals of AUSTRALIA

BOOKS FOR WORLD EXPLORERS
NATIONAL GEOGRAPHIC SOCIETY

Contents

Copyright © 1984 National Geographic Society
Library of Congress CIP Data: page 104

COVER: *A young red kangaroo curls up snug and secure in its mother's pouch. Kangaroos live throughout Australia—one decorates the national coat of arms as a symbol of the continent's unusual wildlife. Young kangaroos are called joeys.*

TOM MCHUGH/PHOTO RESEARCHERS, INC.

TITLE PAGE: *Taking a break, a red kangaroo rests during the hottest part of the day. Kangaroos sometimes dig shallow beds in the desert soil to lie in. Red kangaroos live in central Australia.*

PENNY TWEEDIE
DOROTHY MICHELE NOVICK (ART OPPOSITE)

2

Introduction

In the days when sailing ships were exploring little-known parts of the world, their crews often returned home with stories about the wonders they had seen. Imagine what Europeans must have thought when, in the 1600s and 1700s, sailors returned from a faraway place now called Australia. The sailors reported seeing an animal the size of a greyhound, that had a greyhound's tail, "jumped like a Hare," and left footprints like those of a goat.

Other travelers reported spotting an animal that was "black as the Devil," with "2 horns on its head" and wings, and another animal that had the "beak of a Duck" and the body of an otter, with sharp claws and a flat, furry tail.

Today the kangaroo, the flying fox bat, and the platypus are all familiar animals. You've probably seen them at a zoo or in pictures. But people hearing about these animals for the very first time must have had some pretty strange ideas about them. Soon, however, people around the world came to know these and other odd Australian animals, such as the koala, the echidna, the Tasmanian devil. You can, too. Just keep turning the pages.

The Drifting Continents

Look at a map of the earth as it is today. You'll see seven familiar continents. You'll also notice that Australia lies practically alone—isolated, or cut off, from the landmasses of Europe, Asia, Africa, North and South America, and Antarctica.

Australia hasn't always been isolated, scientists now believe. About 250 million years ago, all the continents were joined together in one supercontinent. The drawings on these pages show how the landmasses might have separated and moved apart. Scientists call this movement continental drift.

Why do continents drift? Our planet is covered with a rocky crust. The crust covers a deep layer of very hot rock called the mantle. Heat in the mantle creates slow, extremely powerful currents. The currents carry huge slabs, or plates, of the crust across the globe. Recently, scientists have used space-age equipment to measure continental drift. They say that Australia and North America move about 1 to $1\frac{1}{2}$ inches (3-4 cm)* farther apart each year.

*Metric figures in this book have been rounded off.

The breakup of the supercontinent all those millions of years ago isolated Australia—and separated the animals on that continent from animals on the other continents.

Animals now found only in Australia once ranged widely across other continents, scientists say. Eventually, the egg-laying and pouched mammals that you will learn about in this book died out in most of the world. Only in Australia and on nearby islands do egg-laying mammals survive. Pouched animals—marsupials—can still be found in North and South America. If you've ever seen an opossum, you've seen a marsupial. But only in Australia did a wide variety of marsupials adapt to the many different environments that exist there.

Free from outside influences, the island continent became a giant wildlife preserve. Over millions of years, long before humans brought in dogs, foxes, rabbits, and sheep, Australia's amazing animals developed into the forms we know today.

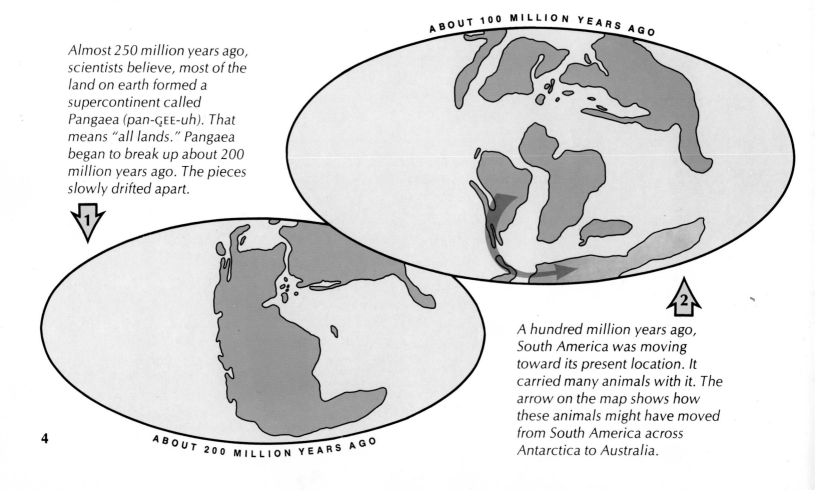

Almost 250 million years ago, scientists believe, most of the land on earth formed a supercontinent called Pangaea (pan-GEE-uh). That means "all lands." Pangaea began to break up about 200 million years ago. The pieces slowly drifted apart.

1 ↓

ABOUT 100 MILLION YEARS AGO

ABOUT 200 MILLION YEARS AGO

2 ↑

A hundred million years ago, South America was moving toward its present location. It carried many animals with it. The arrow on the map shows how these animals might have moved from South America across Antarctica to Australia.

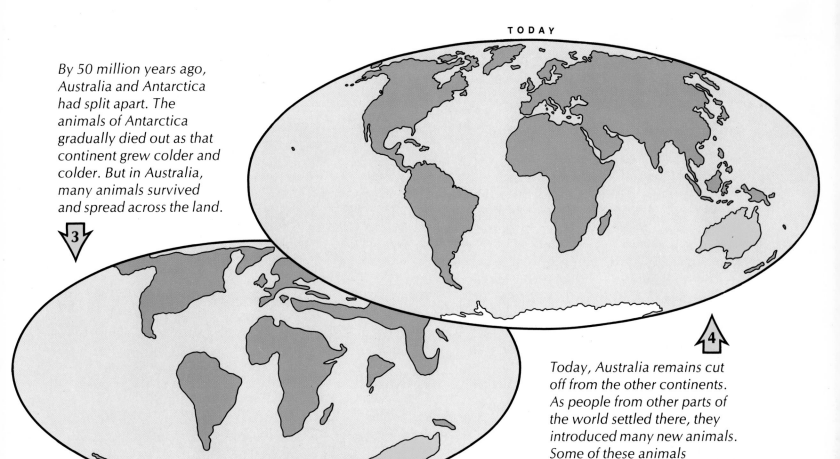

TODAY

By 50 million years ago, Australia and Antarctica had split apart. The animals of Antarctica gradually died out as that continent grew colder and colder. But in Australia, many animals survived and spread across the land.

3 ↓

ABOUT 50 MILLION YEARS AGO

4 ↑

Today, Australia remains cut off from the other continents. As people from other parts of the world settled there, they introduced many new animals. Some of these animals threaten the survival of native Australian animals.

Australia's Mammals

There are three major mammal groups. They are the monotremes (MON-uh-treemz), marsupials (mar-SOO-pea-ulz), and the placentals (pluh-SEN-tulz).

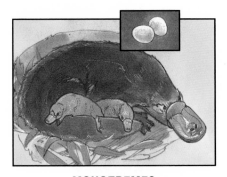

MONOTREMES

MARSUPIALS

PLACENTALS

Mammals called monotremes lay eggs. Platypuses and echidnas are the only monotremes. Their young hatch from eggs, and then get nourishment by sucking milk from pores on the mother's belly.

Marsupials give birth to tiny, underdeveloped young. The young continue to develop, often in pouches, or folds of skin, on their mother's belly. Many Australian mammals belong to this group.

The third kind of mammals, the placentals, give birth to young that have developed inside the mother's body. The many kinds of Australian mice, rats, and bats are placentals.

J. MAUCH (MAPS); MAPS 1, 2, AND 3 ADAPTED FROM MATERIALS PRODUCED BY THE PALEOGEOGRAPHIC ATLAS PROJECT AT THE UNIVERSITY OF CHICAGO   FRANK FRETZ (ART)

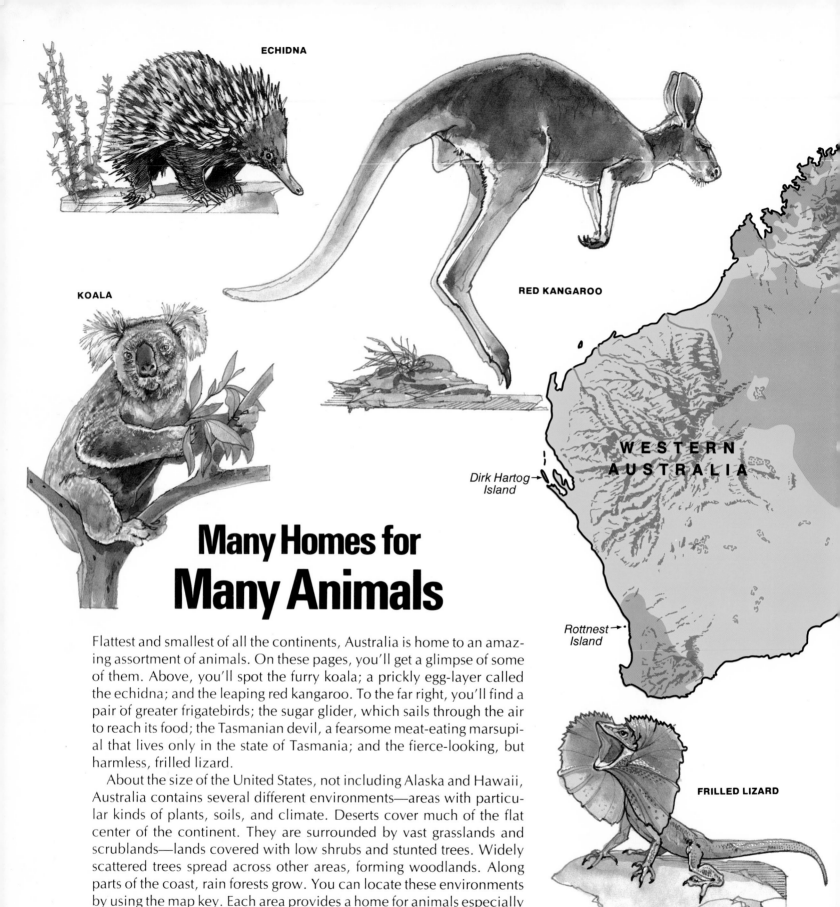

ECHIDNA

KOALA

RED KANGAROO

WESTERN AUSTRALIA

Dirk Hartog Island →

Rottnest Island →

FRILLED LIZARD

Many Homes for
Many Animals

Flattest and smallest of all the continents, Australia is home to an amazing assortment of animals. On these pages, you'll get a glimpse of some of them. Above, you'll spot the furry koala; a prickly egg-layer called the echidna; and the leaping red kangaroo. To the far right, you'll find a pair of greater frigatebirds; the sugar glider, which sails through the air to reach its food; the Tasmanian devil, a fearsome meat-eating marsupial that lives only in the state of Tasmania; and the fierce-looking, but harmless, frilled lizard.

About the size of the United States, not including Alaska and Hawaii, Australia contains several different environments—areas with particular kinds of plants, soils, and climate. Deserts cover much of the flat center of the continent. They are surrounded by vast grasslands and scrublands—lands covered with low shrubs and stunted trees. Widely scattered trees spread across other areas, forming woodlands. Along parts of the coast, rain forests grow. You can locate these environments by using the map key. Each area provides a home for animals especially suited to its conditions. As you read the chapters of this book, you will meet some of the animals that live in these environments.

6

FRANK FRETZ (ART)   PETER J. BALCH (MAP)

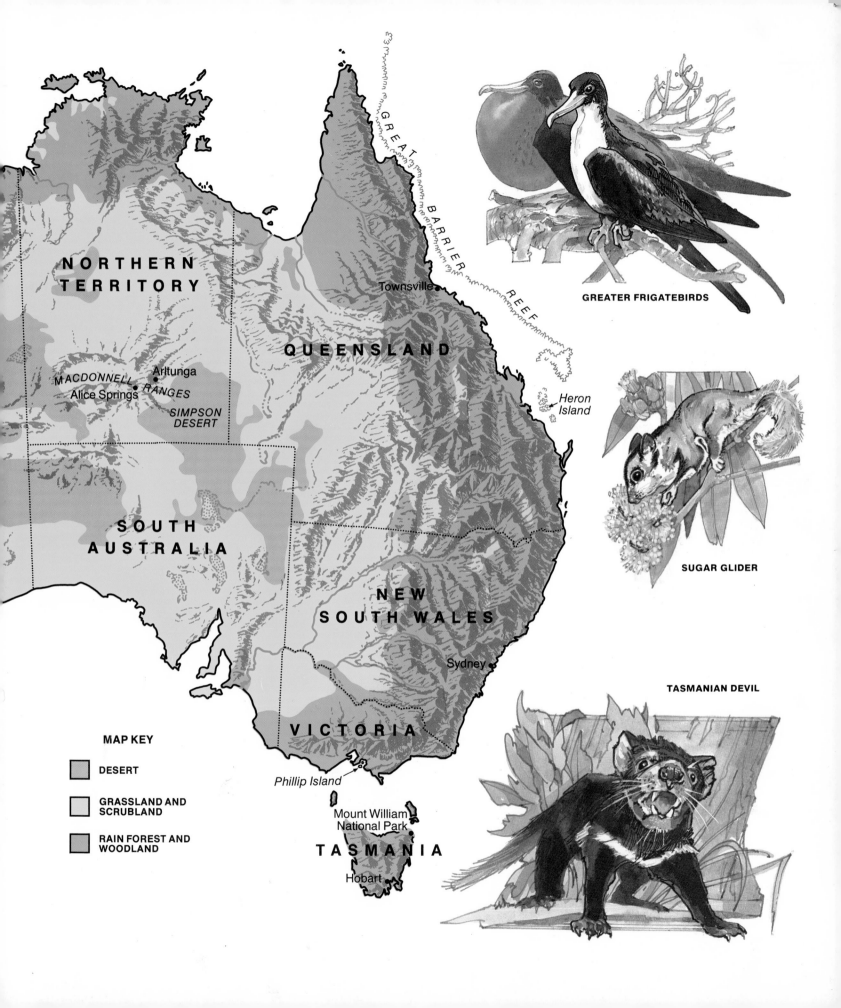

NORTHERN
TERRITORY

QUEENSLAND

MACDONNELL
Arltunga
RANGES
Alice Springs
*SIMPSON
DESERT*

SOUTH
AUSTRALIA

GREAT

BARRIER

REEF

Townsville

Heron
Island

NEW
SOUTH WALES

Sydney

VICTORIA

Phillip Island

Mount William
National Park

TASMANIA

Hobart

MAP KEY

DESERT

GRASSLAND AND
SCRUBLAND

RAIN FOREST AND
WOODLAND

GREATER FRIGATEBIRDS

SUGAR GLIDER

TASMANIAN DEVIL

1. Outback and Scrubland

A spiny anteater, or echidna (ih-KID-nuh), creeps slowly along. It explores the ground with its tube-shaped snout. When it finds ants, it shoots out a long, sticky tongue and scoops up a meal. Echidnas live in dry parts of Australia.

When people in Australia talk about going to the outback, they don't mean that they're going out into the backyard. In Australia, the outback refers to the large dry central part of the continent. Most of Australia is flat and dry, but the vast central plains are the flattest, driest part. Scraggly low plants and stunted trees make up the scrublands, which cover the outskirts of the outback. As you travel inland, toward the center of the country, conditions get drier and drier. The plants and animals found in the outback must be well suited to life in desert conditions in order to survive.

The outback looks lifeless at first glance. Here and there, you see clumps of spiny plants called spinifex (SPY-nuh-fecks), or porcupine grass. Look closer. Near the sharp spinifex stems you may spot a wallaby (WOLL-uh-bee) or a fat-tailed dunnart (DUN-nert), animals with bodies and habits well suited to life in the outback. Beneath a grove of stunted trees you may see a mob, or group, of kangaroos sheltering from the hot sun. In rocky places, snakes and lizards rest in the shadows.

Most of your wildlife-watching in the Australian outback may have to take place after sundown. Many outback creatures are nocturnal. They are active mainly at night.

Clint Bryan is lucky. He is able to see many of Australia's amazing animals up close. Clint lives with his brother Sean, 14, and their parents in the outback near Alice Springs. His father, Ross, works as a park ranger for the Conservation Commission of the Northern Territory. The Bryans live in a thinly settled area. They're familiar with a landscape that may look strange to most people: red, sandy hills . . . thorny, dry plants . . . vast grasslands. On these pages, you'll join the Bryan boys and their father on a trip through some of the dry central parts of their country.

Nice bilby. . . . Clint Bryan, 10, handles a bilby (BILL-bee), or rabbit-eared bandicoot (left). Clint treats it gently. Bilbies are rare. They live in long, spiral-shaped burrows. Sleeping during the day, they come out at night to hunt mice and insects.

Clint and his brother Sean, 14, ride in the back of a truck during a trip through the Macdonnell Ranges, in central Australia (right). Their father, a ranger for the Conservation Commission of the Northern Territory, drives. During their trip, the boys saw many of the animals that live in the dry grasslands and deserts of the outback.

PENNY TWEEDIE (BOTH)

*T*he boys meet a tadpole (above). Their father holds it in his hand. Within days, this tadpole will develop into a water-holding frog. These frogs have an unusual water-storage system. Their skin absorbs moisture. During dry spells, they burrow into the ground, dig a small chamber, and enclose their bodies in a watertight envelope. They breathe through tiny tubes attached to their nostrils.

It was at the Arid Zone Research Institute, just outside Alice Springs, that Clint made friends with a bilby. If Clint had been one of the early European settlers of Australia, he might have kept one of these animals as a pet. They are good at catching mice, and they eat insects, too.

Bilbies, also called rabbit-eared bandicoots (BAN-dih-kootz), are marsupials. That means they give birth to underdeveloped young. The young then continue to grow in a pouch or attached to a teat, or nipple, on their mother's body. Many Australian mammals—including, of course, the kangaroos—are marsupials. About 130 species, or varieties, of marsupials live in Australia.

The Bryans explored the hills of the Macdonnell

*C*lint gets acquainted with a one-year-old red kangaroo (left). This little animal is a pet. It lives with a ranger at Arltunga, a remote ranger station in the Macdonnell Ranges.

13

PENNY TWEEDIE (BOTH)

Ranges, a series of huge rocky outcrops in the heart of Australia. In one of the streams that flow in these hills, Ross Bryan introduced his sons to a tadpole that will develop into a frog unusually well suited to life in the outback. When a rare rainfall hits the desert, this frog absorbs water through its skin. Then it burrows deep into soft clay or sand and enters a sleeplike state. During long dry spells—some as long as two years—the frog remains sealed in its personal waterbag. Only when it rains again does the frog return to the surface.

Another creature has an even more surprising way of surviving in the desert. It catches every drop of available moisture. Its skin carries rain, dew, or surface water to its mouth. This animal is a reptile called a thorny devil.

Scientists discovered how a thorny devil absorbs water by dipping areas of its body in water. If one of the animal's legs gets wet, the thorny devil begins swallowing. That's because the animal has a network of tiny channels on the surface of its skin. The water travels along the channels and gathers in the reptile's mouth. All the devil has to do is swallow. Even the lightest coating of dew can be swallowed using this method.

Clint got a close look at a thorny devil when he and Sean explored some sand hills in the Simpson Desert. Although the little reptile looks fearsome, it's harmless. Thorny devils live in Australia's driest regions. They live on a diet of ants—sometimes as many as several thousand in one meal.

The thorny devil is too slow to escape enemies, but it does have a system of defense. If you were a predator looking for a tasty meal, would you want to swallow an animal covered with spines? The thorny devil also has a thick hump of skin on the back of its neck that may make it look frightening to an animal that tries to attack it.

The Bryans' trip took them through some of the wild places around Alice Springs, in the Northern Territory. The Northern Territory is a self-governing region that covers one-sixth of the Australian continent—an area almost as large as Alaska. Alice Springs, a town about 50 miles (80 km) from the ranger station where the Bryans live, is one of the population centers of the Northern Territory. "The Alice" is almost at the center of Australia. Many people hope that the town may someday become the center of a national park set aside to preserve the natural wonders of the outback. If that happens, the park will shelter large numbers of one of Australia's most familiar animals: the kangaroo.

Horned but harmless, a thorny devil displays its spiny hide (left). This reptile lives in desert areas, surviving on a diet of ants. It relies on its frightening appearance and its prickly skin to protect it from being hunted by other animals.

On a sand hill in the Simpson Desert, Clint watches a thorny devil (right). Earlier, Clint held the scary-looking reptile, then released it. Thorny devils are easy to catch. Unlike other lizards, they move slowly.

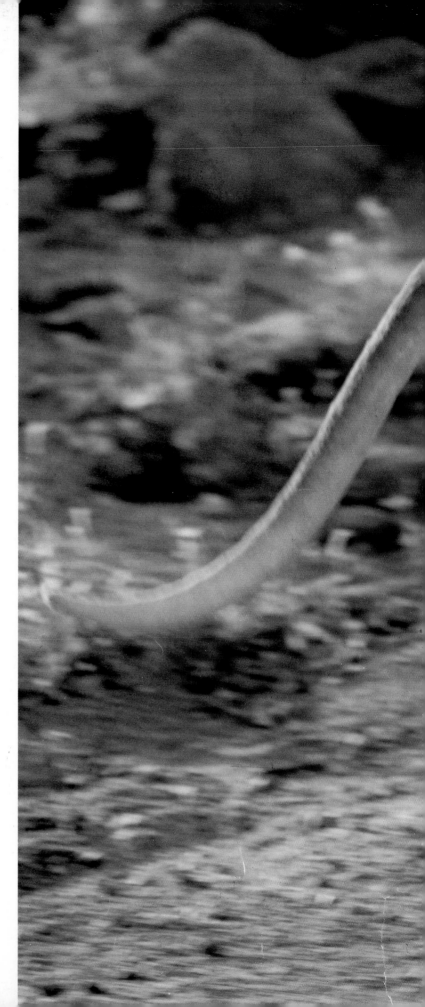

If you were in the outback, visiting a station of the National Parks Service, you might overhear a conversation about boomers, blue fliers, and joeys.

Sounds as if people were discussing nicknames of players on an ice hockey team, doesn't it? But those names are used to describe kangaroos, not athletes. "Boomer" is a nickname for an adult male. "Blue flier" describes an adult female. "Joey" is used for any young kangaroo.

Kangaroos graze in many parts of Australia's outback. Red kangaroos live in the dry center of the continent, traveling widely as they graze. They are good jumpers. At their best, they can cover almost 30 feet (9 m) in one bound. That's about the length of a large school bus.

Red kangaroos are the largest members of a family known by the scientific name *macropodidae* (mac-ruh-PAH-DUH-dee), or "big feet." If you look at the pictures on these pages, you'll see why scientists gave the animals that name.

When kangaroos hop, their hind legs move together. Their muscular tails give balance, and serve as a prop when the animals land. Kangaroos don't

Kangaroos come in all sizes. The drawing above shows the smallest and the largest kangaroos, compared with an average-size man. The tiniest roo, a musky rat kangaroo, is about 6 inches (15 cm) tall. The larger red kangaroo stands at 6 feet (2 m). The man is 5 feet 9 inches (1³/₄ m).

FRANK FRETZ (ART)   PENNY TWEEDIE (RIGHT)

Boing! A red kangaroo bounces along. When a kangaroo moves like this, it covers a lot of ground. At a medium pace, it hops about 6 feet (2 m) with each bounce. If the kangaroo is in a hurry, it leaps as far as 30 feet (9 m) in one bound.

spend all their time hopping, however. When they graze, they crawl on all fours—and look quite awkward to humans. For long-distance travel, kangaroos hop along on their hind legs, covering about 6 feet (2 m) in each jump. If they need to put on a burst of speed, they can move even faster. That's when they make those school-bus-length leaps.

Warm-blooded, covered with fur, and fed on milk from the mother's body, kangaroos are mammals. But they also are marsupials. Young kangaroos spend part of their early life growing in a pouch on the mother's belly.

Scientists once were mystified by the question of how the joey, or young kangaroo, got into its mother's pouch. After careful observation, they found out. Here's what happens:

About a month after a female red kangaroo mates with a male, she gives birth to a single joey. It is tiny—only about the size of a lima bean. This hairless, blind creature has well-developed forelegs.

Making a bed, a female red kangaroo scrapes away the sun-scorched top layer of soil. She exposes a patch of cooler earth below. Soon she will stretch out in the cool, dusty soil for a nap.

During a quarrel—real or just in play—one kangaroo uses its tail as a prop while it tries to kick the other (left). Kangaroos usually live together peacefully. However, males may fight during competition for females.

On a hot day in the outback, a male red kangaroo licks its forelegs. As the moisture evaporates, the kangaroo cools off. Kangaroos also pant to stay cool. During the hottest part of the day, they usually rest. They become most active at dusk.

But its hind legs—the limbs that will eventually grow strong and long enough to push the animal forward in long leaps—have just begun to grow.

To reach the pouch, a joey makes a dangerous journey. It crawls from the birth canal to the pouch through the thick, coarse hair on its mother's belly. The tiny animal makes the 6-inch (15-cm) trip in about 3 minutes. It pulls itself up with its little claws. Hand over hand, it struggles toward the pouch.

When the joey enters the pouch, it searches about for a nipple to attach itself to. Then it begins to drink milk. During the next six months, the young kangaroo will grow . . . and grow . . . and grow . . . until it is large enough to come out of the pouch and begin life on its own. Then it will learn to graze on grass, just as the other kangaroos do.

For a while, the joey continues to drink milk from its mother's body. Even though it may have grown too large to jump into the pouch, it stands in front of its mother, puts its head into her pouch, and drinks. Meanwhile, another immature joey may be inside, starting its period of growth in the safety of the pouch. Kangaroo mothers produce two kinds of milk when they have two young of different ages.

There are stocky, medium-size kangaroos called wallaroos. Still smaller kangaroos, known as wallabies, also inhabit the Australian outback, woodlands, and forests. You'll see some wallaroos and wallabies on the next two pages. They are only a few examples of the different sizes and shapes kangaroos and their relatives may take. In all, some 45 varieties of kangaroos live in Australia. Some are as small as rats, while others—like the red roo—stand taller than an adult human being. With that many kinds of kangaroos living on the land, it's no surprise to discover that the Australians chose the kangaroo as a symbol for their national coat of arms.

Before people came to the continent now called

A young kangaroo spends about six months growing in the safety of its mother's pouch. First, however, it must make a hazardous trip to get there. **(1)** Just after birth, the lima-bean-size joey crawls through the hair on its mother's belly toward her pouch. **(2)** With no help from its mother, the blind, hairless newborn works its way to the pouch using only its forepaws. **(3)** Once inside the pouch, it attaches itself to a nipple and begins to nurse. For many days, it lies curled inside the pouch, drinking milk and growing. After about six months, the little roo will risk going outside.

FRANK FRETZ (ALL ART)

Ready for lunch, a joey stands with its forepaws on the lip of its mother's pouch (above). After it first leaves its mother and begins to graze on its own, the joey returns to the pouch for food and protection.

Australia, kangaroos had little to fear from predators. Some large lizards hunted young kangaroos, as did several birds of prey. In general, however, the large marsupials grazed peacefully. The peace didn't last. Australia's natives, called Aborigines (ab-uh-RIH-juh-neez), introduced a kind of dog called the dingo to the land. Later, Europeans brought foxes to kill the rabbits that ate their crops. Today, dingoes hunt kangaroos, and foxes kill joeys. People hunt kangaroos, too.

Experts disagree on whether kangaroos need protection. Some people say the kangaroo population is threatened. Others say it has grown too large. In some places, farmers insist that kangaroos compete with sheep for grazing areas and should be destroyed. However, many scientists now believe that kangaroos and sheep can graze the same areas without running out of food. The argument over kangaroo management in Australia continues.

Set to flip over and curl up, the joey pushes its head inside the pouch (above). The mother kangaroo stands still while the joey tumbles in.

Safe inside, the joey peers out at the world (above). In the three small drawings, you can see how it got into the "pouch position." The joey enters headfirst. Once inside, it does a forward somersault. Here it ends up curled in a ball, with head, hind legs, and the tip of its tail poking out.

Furry wallaroos stand on their hind legs (above), using their tails as a third leg. Also called euros (YOU-rohs), these animals are members of the kangaroo family called macropodidae, or "big feet." Slightly smaller than red kangaroos, wallaroos are stocky and powerfully built. Some

JEN AND DES BARTLETT (ABOVE AND BELOW)

With long tails trailing behind them, a female unadorned rock wallaby and her joey sit on a boulder (above). These animals use their tails for balance while moving among the rocks. They also have well-padded hind feet for sitting and jumping.

Orange fur rings the eyes of this wallaby (below). It's called a spectacled hare wallaby. Once these small marsupials occurred in great numbers. Today, only scattered populations remain on the mainland.

inhabit rocky areas and mountainous zones of Australia. Their broad feet help prevent them from slipping on rocks.

In the outback, you may be lucky enough to see a curious sight. In a clearing, you might spot a huge, shaggy-feathered bird sitting on a nest full of dark green eggs. When the bird stands up, it probably would tower over you. It's an emu (EE-mew), the second-biggest bird on earth. This large bird often stands as tall as 6 feet (2 m). With the kangaroo, the emu shares the honor of appearing on Australia's national coat of arms.

Slightly smaller than an ostrich, the emu is Australia's largest bird. Although it can run at 30 miles an hour (48 km/h), it can't fly at all. Over many generations, as the bird gradually grew in height and developed long legs for speed, its wings became smaller. Finally, they became useless.

Emus live over much of the Australian mainland. They gather in flocks to feed and sometimes anger farmers by knocking down fences and eating crops.

At breeding time, the female emu lays large eggs, each weighing 1 1/2 to 2 pounds (1/2-1 kg). The female pays little attention to the eggs. The male spends eight weeks sitting on the nest. After the chicks hatch, he watches over them for the next 18 months, as they grow.

© JEAN-PAUL FERRERO

Moving gently, a male emu tends a nest full of green eggs (above). After the female emu lays the eggs, the male takes over. He hatches them and takes care of the chicks.

A flock of emus races through a field (below). These huge birds run fast—as fast as 30 miles an hour (48 km/h)—and far. But they can't fly.

Big bird! An emu—the largest bird in Australia, and the second largest on earth—opens its powerful beak. Emus eat almost anything. Their normal diet includes leaves, grass, fruit, flowers, and insects. They need a lot of food. Large male emus weigh about 120 pounds (54 kg).

25

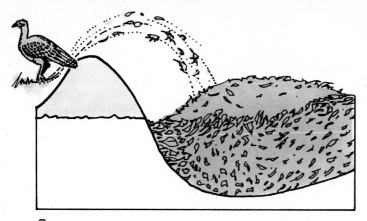

1 *In the fall, a male mallee fowl begins the task of building a nesting mound. Digging a large hole, he fills it with dry leaves and twigs.*

If you take a walk through the scrubland of Australia and come upon a large mound of sand and leaves, take care. That's not a trash pile. It's a nursery for the eggs of the mallee (MAH-lee) fowl. Under the sand, chicks are growing inside their eggs.

Most birds sit on their eggs to warm them as the chicks develop. But not the mallee fowl. This bird uses other sources of heat.

If you have a compost heap in your garden, you know that vegetation produces heat as it rots. Within the mallee fowl's mound, a pile of rotting leaves and twigs acts as an incubator to warm the eggs.

The sandpile above the eggs serves as insulation. The male mallee fowl controls the temperature inside the mound. It's a full-time job. He may have to adjust the depth of the sandpile several times a day to control the temperature inside the mound.

The male mallee fowl's day begins just after sunrise. He thrusts his beak into the mound. Sensitive cells on the tongue "read" the temperature.

In the spring, when the rotting leaves produce the most heat, the bird scratches some of the sand away, letting heat escape. During the summer, he adds more sand, to protect the eggs from the sun's rays. In autumn, when the inner heat has died down, he opens the eggs to the sun.

The mallee fowl tends his mound for about seven weeks before the first chick hatches. With no help from its parents, the young mallee fowl must struggle through the sand to the surface, and begin life.

2 *After winter rains soak the leaves and twigs, the male scoops an egg chamber in the mound. He fills it with sand and leaves, and covers the mound with sandy soil. As the leaves rot, they will heat up.*

3 *When the female is ready to lay her first egg, the male scrapes away the sand, exposing the egg chamber. Then he tests the mound with his sensitive tongue to make sure it is just the right temperature.*

4 *With her mate close by, the female deposits an egg in the hole he has dug. The male then covers the egg. The female will return about once a week to lay more eggs, until she has laid about 18.*

A pair of mallee fowl stand atop their mound (above). Once the female lays her eggs, the male busies himself with the task of keeping the mound at a steady 92°F (33° C). He will remove or add sand to maintain that temperature. In the late summer, the leaves may not produce enough heat. During the day, he may scrape off the layer of sand so the sun can warm the eggs.

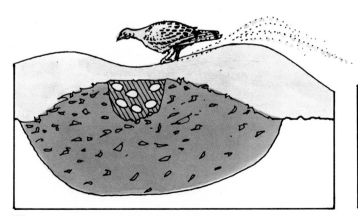

5 While the eggs develop, the male tends the mound daily. He scrapes away sand or adds it, balancing the heat produced by the decaying vegetation with that of the sun.

6 About seven weeks after it was laid, the first egg hatches. The chick must struggle up through about 3 feet (1 m) of sand. It arrives at the surface fully feathered. After a rest, it goes off to begin life.

27

Throughout Australia, you might spot a small, spiny animal creeping along, looking for ants or termites to eat. If you approach one as it walks among rocks, it rolls up into a tight ball to defend itself. If you try to investigate it on a sandy path, the animal suddenly digs down into the earth and disappears.

The animal is a short-nosed echidna, or spiny anteater. The echidna belongs to one of the most ancient of mammal groups, the monotremes (MON-uh-treemz). Another kind of echidna, called the long-nosed echidna, lives in New Guinea. Animals similar to the echidna have lived in Australia for millions of years.

Like other mammals, echidnas are warm-blooded, have hair, and nurse their young with milk from their bodies. But echidnas do one unusual thing. They lay eggs. Only one other mammal lays eggs. It lives in Australia, too, and it is called the platypus (PLAT-ih-pus). You can read more about it on page 72. Echidnas and platypuses are the world's only surviving monotremes.

An echidna mother carries her single egg about with her in a pouch-like flap of skin on her belly. When the young hatches, it sucks milk from pores on the mother's skin. After carrying her young in her pouch for about eight weeks, the mother forces it out. It has begun to grow spines and is an uncomfortable package to carry. She hides it in a hollow log or among rocks, returning regularly to feed it. Soon, the little echidna begins to hunt for its own food.

Echidnas live on ants and termites that they lap up with their long, sticky tongues. They are very strong. When they're hunting for a meal, they may push over large rocks to search for hidden insects.

The echidna does its disappearing act when it feels threatened. It has no teeth with which to bite an enemy. Instead, it relies on its spines and its strength to stay alive. If disturbed, it uses its four powerful, clawed feet to dig straight down into the earth. In a matter of minutes, the animal almost disappears. Only a few spines show above the ground.

A young echidna lies curled in a flap of skin on its mother's belly (left). It won't be there much longer. Its spines have begun to appear. Once they start poking the mother, she will put the young echidna in a hollow log or among rocks and care for it there.

JEN AND DES BARTLETT (LEFT)

Nobody bothers an echidna (below). This one rolls up in self-defense. An enemy trying to bite into its soft belly would have a painful experience.

© JEAN-PAUL FERRERO

Surprised on soft ground, an echidna puts on a disappearing act (above). It digs straight down with its four powerful feet. In minutes, it is safely buried. Only a few spines stick above the surface—and they could easily be mistaken for grass.

G. WEBER/NATIONAL PHOTOGRAPHIC INDEX (AUSTRALIA) (LEFT)

In disguise, a green stick insect hangs upside down on a twig. Its resemblance to a stick helps protect it from enemies. To a predator, the insect may look like part of a plant. As the drawing below shows, these creatures are among the largest insects in the world. This one is about 10 inches (25 cm) long.

MICHAEL AND IRENE MORCOMBE

FRANK FRETZ (ART)

Around the world, millions upon millions of insects buzz, scurry, and swarm. In Australia, you would see many insects that look familiar: bees, ants, grasshoppers, and butterflies. You'd also run across some unusual insects native to Australia.

Meet two kinds of Australian insects that have developed different ways of surviving: the stick insect and the bulldog ant.

The stick insect has no attack system. Not a hunter, it lives on a diet of leaves. But it does have a defense system. The stick insect looks like a twig. Few enemies can spot it in the foliage in which it lives.

The bulldog ant uses an attack system to hunt other insects and to protect its nest. It has strong jaws to grab its enemies, and strong poison to kill them. In Australia, it takes sharp eyes to avoid the bulldog ant—and even sharper eyes to spot the stick insect.

Sawtooth jaws (right) enable a bulldog ant to hold tight to its prey. The inch-long (2½-cm) insect (below) uses its jaws to grab other insects. It stuns the prey with poison injected with a stinger. Then the ant carries the meal to the rest of the colony, which is hidden safely underground.

31

The animals called mammals are well equipped to stay warm. Mammals are warm-blooded. Their bodies maintain about the same temperature even if the temperature around them changes.

Reptiles don't have this advantage. Reptiles are cold-blooded. Their body temperature changes as the temperature of the air changes.

Have you ever seen a lizard basking on a sun-warmed rock? Lizards are reptiles. They rely on heat from the sun to keep warm. So it's not surprising that many of the world's reptiles live in warm, sunny places—like Australia.

All reptiles have some things in common. They have scales, they're cold-blooded, and their bodies lie close to the ground. In spite of these similarities, reptiles come in an amazing variety of shapes, colors, and sizes. In Australia, you can spot a small, spine-covered thorny devil, or a huge, smooth-scaled perentie (puh-REN-tee).

Few countries shelter as many different types of reptiles as Australia does. You can find more than 150 different kinds of small lizards called skinks. You'll see two different skinks on the next page. About a hundred kinds of snakes also live in Australia. More than half are poisonous, although only a few have poison powerful enough to be dangerous to people.

Some snakes use poison to defend themselves. Large reptiles like perenties rely on size for defense. Other reptiles have developed different ways of staying safe. Some have skin that blends well with their surroundings, providing camouflage. When the animal stops moving, it seems to disappear. The enemy hunting it often walks right by.

Other reptiles use bluff. They puff themselves up, hiss, and stand on their hind legs. Or they may display parts of their bodies to make themselves look larger than they are—as the frilled lizard does.

Still others, like many of the geckos, have tails that break off. If an enemy grabs a gecko, the little reptile drops its tail. The gecko rushes to safety while the wriggling tail distracts the predator.

JEAN-PAUL FERRERO/ARDEA LONDON

Coiled on a tree stump, a desert death adder waits for prey (right). This dangerously poisonous snake lives in the red sand desert areas of central Australia. When the adder is hungry, it wriggles the end of its tail. Other reptiles and small mammals, mistaking the wriggling tail for an insect, become the snake's meal.

Lidless eyes and a stumpy tail identify the reptile at left as a knob-tailed gecko. This little lizard uses its tongue as a windshield wiper to clean its eyes. If alarmed, it will puff itself up and make threatening noises before running to safety.

MICHAEL AND IRENE MORCOMBE (ABOVE AND OPPOSITE)

Keep away! A frilled lizard strikes a scary pose atop a termite mound. It raises its frill, puffs up its body, and opens its mouth. If that doesn't scare intruders away, this reptile, which may grow 3 feet (1 m) long, stands on its hind legs and runs to safety.

What looks like a cross between a snake and a lizard? A skink (above). About 150 kinds of skinks live in Australia. This glossy-skinned, tiny-legged skink spends most of its time in a burrow under a stone or a log. It lives on insects.

A blue-tongued skink sticks out the tongue that gives it its name (above). This harmless reptile grows 1 1/2 feet (1/2 m) long. If a blue-tongued skink feels threatened, it opens its mouth, hisses slowly, and shows its tongue. This startles the attacker while the skink tries to make a getaway.

Australia's largest lizard, a perentie crawls up a rocky outcrop in central Australia (right). This huge lizard, also called a goanna (go-AHN-uh), or monitor, may grow 8 feet (2 2/5 m) long. It uses its sharp teeth to eat lizards, birds, and small mammals such as rabbits and mice. The perentie may also lash out at enemies with its powerful tail.

Only a few kinds of mammals lived on the continent now called Australia before the first humans arrived. Bats, echidnas, native mice and rats, platypuses, and marsupials had the continent to themselves. Few enemies disturbed them.

About 40,000 years ago, however, the Aborigines arrived, bringing a new mammal with them. It was a dog called the dingo. Because the mammals of Australia had not yet developed ways of defending themselves against dingoes, these new predators had an easy time finding food. Descendants of those first dingoes, many of them now roaming wild, remain a major predator of other Australian mammals.

In the late 1700s, Europeans came, bringing many other new animals. They brought rabbits, which multiplied so fast that they began eating much of the wild vegetation—and the farmers' crops. Then the Europeans introduced foxes. The foxes hunted the rabbits, but they also preyed on native animals such as the quokka.

Domestic cats also arrived with the Europeans. Some of the cats escaped and began to hunt small native animals such as the fat-tailed dunnart. No one really knows the effect these cats had as predators, but some people think they caused the decline of several smaller mammals.

Today, in spite of these newcomers, many Australian marsupials thrive, as the kangaroo appears to be doing. On Rottnest Island, off the western coast, quokkas hop around freely. On this island, there are no foxes to hunt them. Human development, however, may soon threaten their habitat. And on the mainland, quokkas have become quite rare.

New kinds of animals, and the changes brought to the land by humans, have reduced the ranges of some native Australian animals. But in many parts of the outback, a curious explorer can still see many animals that have changed little since the time the Aborigines came. In some places, Australian wildlife experts have set aside protected areas and parks where the animals live safely in their native land.

This marsupial (above) carries a lunch box in its tail. A fat-tailed dunnart stores extra fat in its tail. When food becomes scarce, it lives on the fat. About the size of a house mouse, the dunnart is a fierce night hunter. It lives mostly on insects.

In a field of flowers, a quokka stands on its hind legs (right). The quokka is a kind of short-tailed, short-eared wallaby. A marsupial, it raises its young in a pouch. This quokka lives on Rottnest Island, off the west coast of Australia. Although hunted by foxes, a few quokkas survive on the Australian mainland.

2. Sea and Shore

These playful marine mammals, called Australian sea lions, find the coast of South Australia an ideal spot for living and for raising their young. Scientists think they spend their entire lives near the beach where they were born.

39

Wearing a face mask and a snorkel, you glide through warm, crystal-clear waters along the northeast coast. Below, you see rocklike formations tinted purple, green, yellow, pink. Strange, brightly colored fish swim by. After sunset, you sit on a beach and watch a giant green turtle lumber ashore to lay her eggs. Far to the south, you visit another beach, where the world's smallest penguins breed. Does all this sound like something you'd like to do? You could if you visited the coasts of Australia.

Australia's seacoast stretches for more than 22,000 miles (35,405 km). It is home to many animals. Some of them also live in other parts of the world. Others are found only in Australia.

The Australian sea lion, for example, lives nowhere else in the world. From 3,000 to 5,000 Australian sea lions inhabit islands off the southern and southwestern coasts.

An underwater wonderland borders the coast of northeast Australia. It is the Great Barrier Reef—the largest group of coral reefs in the world. Together, the reefs extend 1,250 miles (2,012 km) and cover an area about as large as the countries of England and Scotland combined.

Coral reefs result from the slow growth of animals called stony corals. These corals are tiny—only a fraction of an inch in diameter. A single coral forms a colony, or group, by making hundreds, even thousands, of copies of itself. As a colony grows upward and sideways, it produces a rocklike skeleton. More colonies begin to grow when new coral animals attach themselves to the skeletons of dead corals and begin to duplicate themselves. Very slowly, the reef grows. The Great Barrier Reef has been forming for tens of millions of years.

Over time, wind and waves deposit crushed coral and shells on top of a reef, and form a low island called a cay (KEY). Nesting birds fertilize the cay with their droppings. Birds, winds, and water bring seeds. Eventually, some seeds grow into plants.

The South Pacific Ocean borders the east coast of Australia, the Indian Ocean the west coast.

Heron Island (left), one of many coral islands called cays, lies atop Heron Reef, at the southern end of the Great Barrier Reef. At a research station here, scientists are trying to find ways to protect the reefs and the many forms of wildlife they shelter.

Silvery fish called trevally search the water for food dropped by two snorkelers (right). Jonathan Heighes, 9, right, and Justine McIllree, 11, both of New South Wales, found the fish off Heron Island. "I could touch them—and did," says Jonathan.

VALERIE TAYLOR (BOTH)

If you went snorkeling off the shores of a Great Barrier Reef cay, what would you see? Some people say the reefs themselves look like underwater gardens. Hundreds of kinds of reef-building corals live in the warm waters of the reefs. The corals grow in a variety of shapes, sizes, and colors. Some colonies are as big as buses.

Some kinds of coral cover reefs but don't build them. These corals, called soft coral, resemble bunches of flowers.

The reefs themselves shelter many sea creatures. One reef alone may contain more than a thousand different kinds of plants and animals. Near a large clump of coral, called a coral head or a bommie, you may see thousands of colorful tropical fish. They feed on plankton, tiny floating plants and animals. Plankton is the main food source for many animals. When danger threatens, the animals dart to safety within the coral structures.

If you found an anemonefish (uh-NEM-uh-nee-fish) in its home, you might be amazed at where it lives. The anemonefish, a small, brightly colored fish, shares a strange relationship with another animal called a sea anemone. The sea anemone has stinging tentacles that paralyze many small reef-dwelling fish, but anemonefish snuggle among the tentacles unharmed. Experts now think that these fish have a natural coating on their bodies that makes the anemone unable to detect their presence.

One of the reef's most colorful residents is the harlequin (HAR-lih-kwun) tusk fish. Its striped body gives this fish its name. A harlequin is a kind of clown. The fish has teeth that look like little tusks. About 10 inches (25 cm) long, the harlequin tusk fish uses its teeth like pliers to grab small shellfish.

Another unusual reef-dweller is the nudibranch (NOOD-uh-brank), or sea slug. It feeds on sponges, corals, and the stinging tentacles of anemones and hydroids. The sea slug stores the stinging cells in its own body. It uses them to sting attackers.

Like sparkling fireworks, orange fairy basslets swim around a clump of coral called a coral head (left). The small fish live in cracks in the coral head. They feed on tiny plants and animals called plankton.

Rarely seen by divers, the red Indian fish (above) seems to wear an American Indian headdress. This Australian fish lives in an aquarium in Sydney.

A soft coral waves in the current (below). The members of this animal colony have extended their tentacles to catch plankton. Many kinds of soft corals live in Great Barrier Reef waters.

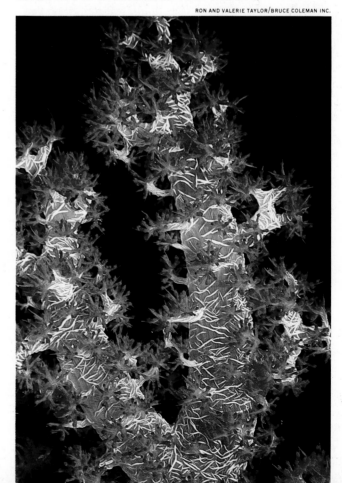

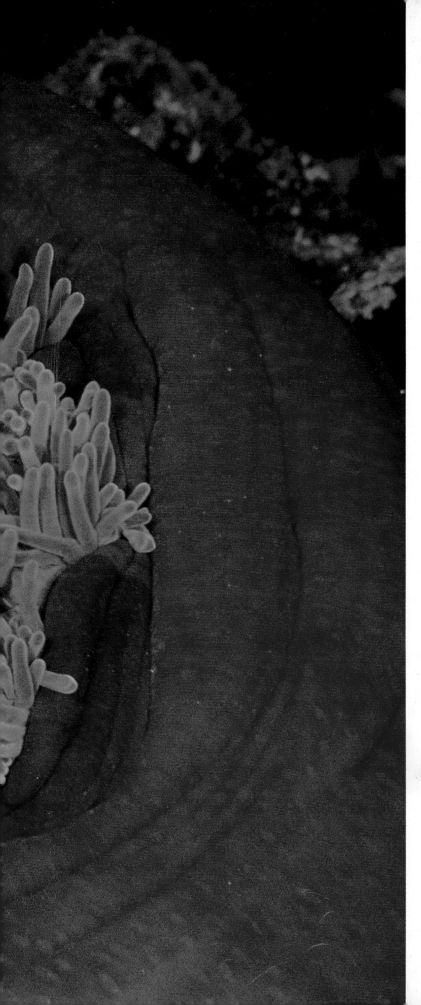

VALERIE TAYLOR/ARDEA LONDON

Blue teeth? The harlequin tusk fish (above) has them. This colorful fish uses its teeth to pick up bottom-dwelling shellfish such as crabs and shrimps. In Australia, the harlequin tusk fish lives among the reefs along the northeastern shore.

Like an underwater ballerina, a reef-dwelling nudibranch, or sea slug, glides through the water (above). Its bright colors may signal that it is poisonous or bad-tasting, and so frighten away possible enemies.

Snug and secure, reef-dwelling anemonefish nestle among a sea anemone's tentacles (left). The tentacles contain stinging cells that paralyze most small fish, but they don't harm the anemonefish.

45

BILL WOOD/AUSTRALIAN PICTURE LIBRARY (LEFT AND ABOVE)

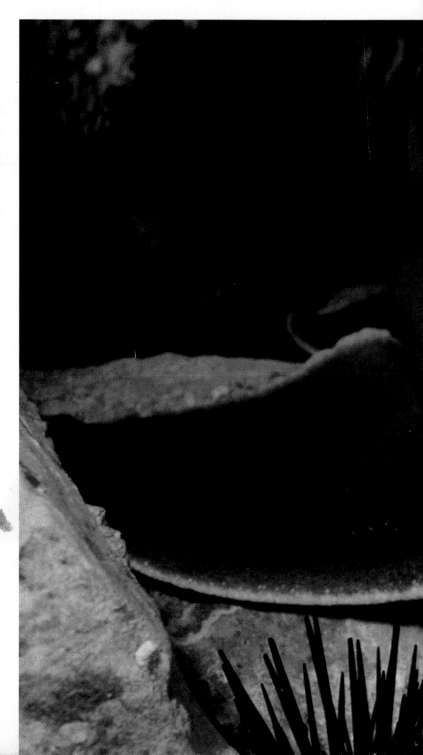

Ho hum. Just resting on the seafloor seems to suit the Port Jackson shark (below). Port Jackson sharks don't attack humans, but they often raid oyster beds off the coast of the state of Tasmania. The sharks come near shore only to lay their eggs.

The slow-moving tasseled wobbegong shark (above) ignores the photographer. But when a crab or an octopus passes within striking distance, the wobbegong snaps it up with one swift motion.

Fish of all shapes and sizes swim in Australian waters. Among the largest are the sharks. About 100 kinds live there. One of the most unusual, the tasseled wobbegong (WAH-be-gahng), lives along the Great Barrier Reef. Although it grows about 10 feet (3 m) long, you might swim right by one without noticing, because it usually rests on the bottom. Its head has fleshy fringes that look like seaweed. Patterns on its body disguise it on the seafloor.

On the other hand, you probably would spot another shark—the hammerhead—from far away. This shark has a long flat lobe on each side of its head. Each lobe has an eye and a nostril at the end. True to its name, the hammerhead shark looks from

M outh open, a hammerhead shark glides over a coral reef (right). Its eyes and nostrils are located at either end of the long, flat lobe, or hammer, on its head. Hammerheads, like most fish, have several sets of teeth. When it loses a tooth, another moves in from behind to replace it.

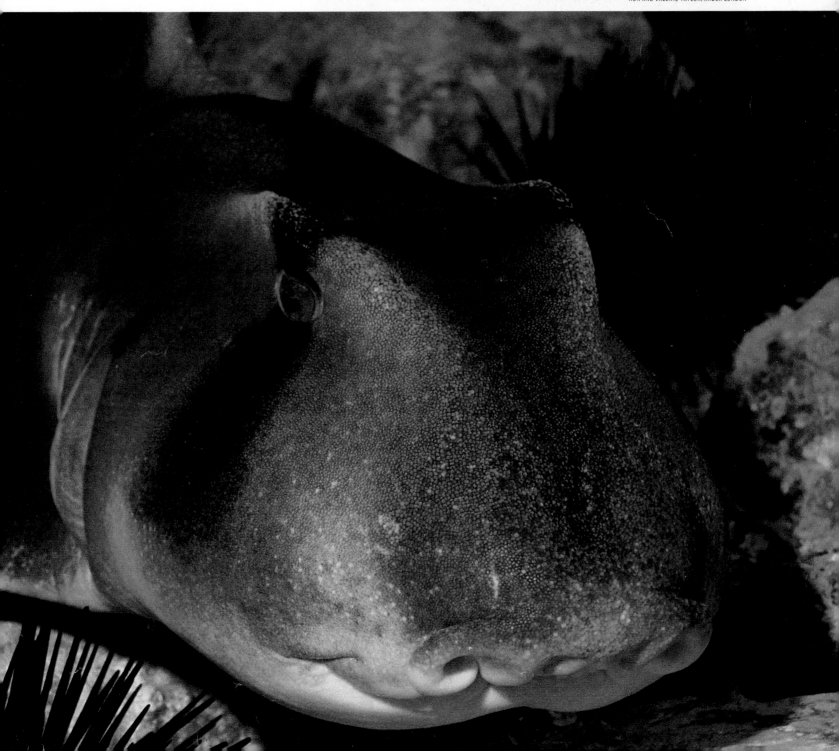

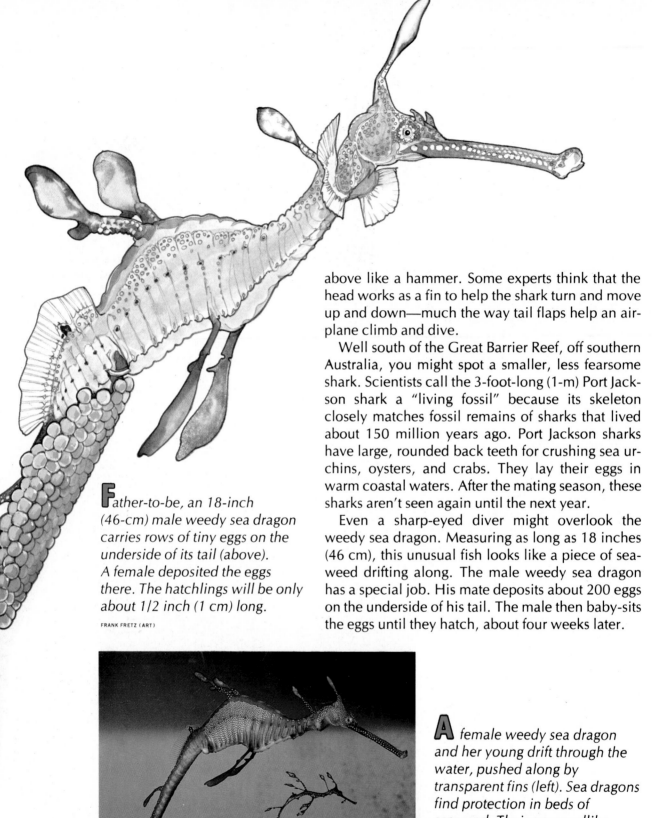

above like a hammer. Some experts think that the head works as a fin to help the shark turn and move up and down—much the way tail flaps help an airplane climb and dive.

Well south of the Great Barrier Reef, off southern Australia, you might spot a smaller, less fearsome shark. Scientists call the 3-foot-long (1-m) Port Jackson shark a "living fossil" because its skeleton closely matches fossil remains of sharks that lived about 150 million years ago. Port Jackson sharks have large, rounded back teeth for crushing sea urchins, oysters, and crabs. They lay their eggs in warm coastal waters. After the mating season, these sharks aren't seen again until the next year.

Even a sharp-eyed diver might overlook the weedy sea dragon. Measuring as long as 18 inches (46 cm), this unusual fish looks like a piece of seaweed drifting along. The male weedy sea dragon has a special job. His mate deposits about 200 eggs on the underside of his tail. The male then baby-sits the eggs until they hatch, about four weeks later.

Father-to-be, an 18-inch (46-cm) male weedy sea dragon carries rows of tiny eggs on the underside of its tail (above). A female deposited the eggs there. The hatchlings will be only about 1/2 inch (1 cm) long.

FRANK FRETZ (ART)

A female weedy sea dragon and her young drift through the water, pushed along by transparent fins (left). Sea dragons find protection in beds of seaweed. Their seaweedlike shape helps protect them from predators.

RUDIE H. KUITER

Not all Australian sea creatures live in the sea. Many nest on the shore. One seabird, the greater frigatebird, has a colorful way of courting. The male, about 3 feet (1 m) long, puffs up a red pouch on his throat. The throat pouch swells to the size of a grapefruit. The male continues to inflate the pouch until he attracts a mate and she lays an egg. Greater frigatebirds nest in trees or bushes. Both parents care for the egg and later for the chick. Although the birds feed on fish and squid, they don't enter the water. Skilled fliers, they swoop down and catch food near the surface. They also rob other seabirds of their food—often snatching it in midair.

The shorter winged pied cormorant feeds in a different way. To get its dinner, it swims underwater, thrusting its long, curved neck as it hunts for fish. When it comes back to the surface, it has a tasty meal in its bill.

Mate wanted! That's what the inflated red throat pouch (above) of this male greater frigatebird signals. The pouch helps attract a mate. When the birds mate and the female produces an egg, the male no longer inflates his pouch.

Preparing to land, a male greater frigatebird brings food to its chick. Greater frigatebird parents take turns feeding and guarding their one chick. With an average wingspan of about 6 feet (2 m), these birds often glide on air currents to conserve energy.

Home from the sea, two fairy penguins meet on the beach (right). After putting their feathers in order, they will head for their burrows, where their mates and young wait.

A pied cormorant pops out of the water with dinner in its bill (below). This bird has a huge appetite. To get a meal, it dives from the surface and swims underwater, using its feet as paddles.

There are even Australian seabirds that can't fly. These are the fairy penguins, the world's smallest penguins—and the only penguins that breed in Australia. Fairy penguins stand about 13 inches (33 cm) tall. They weigh less than 3 pounds (1 kg). To avoid eagles, large seagulls, and other birds that feed in the daytime, fairy penguins come ashore only after dark and only during mating season.

The penguins nest on shore in burrows or in hollows under rocks. The female usually lays two eggs. For the first few weeks after the eggs hatch, the parents take turns providing food for the family. On one day, the female fishes and shares her catch with the chicks. On the next, the male does the fishing.

On Phillip Island, off the southern coast of Victoria, an audience of curious people waits behind fences to watch the penguins parade out of the surf. The returning birds gather at the water's edge. Then, like sailors home from the sea, they move up the beach in groups of eight to ten. Flapping their wings and yapping loudly, each seems to announce, "I'm home!" Their mates and chicks in the burrows excitedly yap back. The lively chatter from the burrows fills the beach all night long. Fairy penguins are Australia's only native penguins. When nesting season is over, the penguins live at sea.

Another animal that nests on some Australian beaches is the green turtle. This reptile, which

RON AND VALERIE TAYLOR/ARDEA LONDON

Ready to nest, a female green turtle makes a pit on a Great Barrier Reef island. With her flippers, she digs sand from under her body and pushes it aside. Then she scoops out a deeper pit called an egg chamber with her hind flippers.

RON AND VALERIE TAYLOR/BRUCE COLEMAN INC.

Carefully, the turtle deposits her eggs in the egg chamber. After laying from 60 to 200 leathery eggs, she refills the chamber and the pit with sand. She may return several times during the nesting season.

weighs 300 pounds (136 kg), spends most of its time at sea. The female makes nighttime trips ashore every three to seven years to lay her eggs. She returns to the same beach where she herself was born. Although a graceful swimmer, the turtle moves slowly and awkwardly on land. Safely beyond the high tide mark, she chooses a nesting site. Then she begins to dig. Using her flippers, she makes a saucer-shaped pit. With her back flippers, she digs a smaller pit, or egg chamber, for her eggs. The eggs feel like leather and look like Ping-Pong balls. She may lay from 60 to 200 eggs in one night. When her job is done, she covers the eggs with sand and crawls slowly back to the sea. The female may return every few weeks for several months to lay eggs.

After about eight weeks, the eggs hatch and the young turtles dig their way out of the nest. They crawl to the sea. There, fish will eat many of them. The older a turtle grows, the better its chances for survival. By the time it reaches its full growth, only sharks will attack it.

At one time, many people in Australia caught green turtles for food. Experts feared that the turtle population was declining. In 1950, Queensland passed the first law banning the commercial hunting of these sea creatures. Today only Australia's native peoples are permitted to hunt them.

In 1979, Australia took steps to protect an even greater national treasure—the Great Barrier Reef. The government set aside a 4,556-square-mile (11,800-km^2) area as a marine park. As a result, if you ever decide to go snorkeling in Australia, you'll see much the same wonderland of life that the first underwater explorers found.

GEORGE HOLTON/PHOTO RESEARCHERS, INC.

Her job done, a 300-pound (136-kg) green turtle paddles out to sea. In about eight weeks, the hatchlings will break out of the eggs. Together, the young will dig through the sand to the surface and head for the sea. Great numbers of sea turtles nest on the islands of the Great Barrier Reef. During nesting season, several thousand females come ashore on some beaches to lay their eggs.

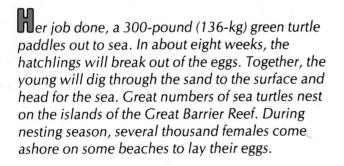

VALERIE TAYLOR

With a human escort, a green turtle heads for the water. The youngsters—from the left, Justine McIllree, Hayden Poole, 11, Jonathan Heighes, and Fiona Jones, 13, all of New South Wales—found the turtle on Heron Island. "She had taken too long to lay her eggs. The tide went out and left her. We were helping her find her way back to the ocean," says Justine. "Eventually she reached it," Hayden adds.

3. Rain Forest and Woodland

A mossy branch provides a narrow walkway for a Herbert River ring-tailed possum. This high-climbing marsupial spends most of its life in the leafy tree-tops of the rain forests and woodlands of Australia.

Woodlands and tropical rain forests (green) grow mostly on Australia's eastern and northern coasts. They also are found in the island-state of Tasmania.

Hidden in the dense trees of the rain forest live many of Australia's most unusual animals. Here, along mountain slopes, evergreen trees tower more than 100 feet (30 m). Their leafy tops form a thick green canopy, or covering, that completely shuts out the sunlight. If you visited such a rain forest, you'd find the ground littered with leaves and twigs. Looking up, you'd see tall tree trunks draped with hanging vines and ferns. High above, you'd see the canopy itself. On your skin, you'd feel moisture, for a rain forest receives a lot of rain.

Along the edges of the rain forest are areas called woodlands. Here the trees usually are shorter and spread farther apart. Between them, sunlight filters down, allowing grass and shrubs to grow.

Rain forests and woodlands support a variety of animals that depend on them for food and shelter. In the rain forest, some animals climb about the leafy canopy, rarely leaving their high homes. In the woodlands, some animals spend their time both in trees and in the grassy areas between the trees. A few woodland dwellers dig underground burrows.

Tree-dwelling marsupials called possums live comfortably in both rain forests and woodlands. Possums move through the treetops feeding on leaves and insects. With feet that grip like hands, possums climb well. Their tails, sometimes longer than their bodies, wrap around branches to give the animals a better grip. Ring-tailed possums are named for their strongly prehensile (pre-HEN-sul), or gripping, tails.

When early explorers first saw these animals,

Hearty eater, a spotted cuscus (KUSS-kuss) munches a piece of fruit (left). This marsupial is about the size of a cat. It moves slowly through the treetops at night, feeding on leaves, fruits, and insects. Occasionally it creeps up on a lizard or a small bird.

Patches of white mark the thick, woolly coat of a spotted cuscus (right). This round-faced animal has a yellowish nose and bulging yellow eyes. The cuscus uses the scaly tip of its tail as an extra hand. Its climbing ability, wide-eyed look, and short ears cause some people to mistake cuscuses for monkeys.

B uilt for burrowing, a common, or coarse-haired, wombat waddles on short, powerful legs. Wombats use mostly their strong front paws to dig tunnels. They may dig several connecting rooms. For sleeping, they carpet one or more of the rooms near the burrow entrance with a nest of plant material.

they named them after a similar pouched animal found in America called the opossum. Then, scientists learned that the two groups of animals were from different families. So scientists dropped the first "o" from the name of the Australian animal.

Possums come in many sizes. The tiny pygmy possum often moves into abandoned birds' nests. It may feed on the juices of flowers larger than its own body. The cuscus, a possum about the size of a cat, hides by moving slowly through the forest heights.

In the rain forests, possums are so at home in the treetops that they rarely come down. In the woodlands, however, many spend time on the ground crossing from one tree to another or even stopping to feed. Like many forest-dwellers, possums are nocturnal. They feed at night. During the day, some possums sleep in nests made of leaves and twigs. Many curl up in hollow branches or tree trunks.

A cuscus may even sleep sitting up on a limb.

Snakes, large lizards, and owls prey on possums. If threatened by an enemy, the cuscus may strike with its sharp front claws. It may snarl and bark. The brush-tailed possum hisses. Then it rises up on its hind legs and screams to frighten an enemy away. If caught, many kinds of possums fight fiercely.

Some members of Australia's kangaroo family also live in the woodlands. Two kinds even climb in the trees of the rain forest. Tree kangaroos look somewhat like their earthbound relatives, but their bodies are built for climbing. Tree kangaroos have shorter, stronger hind legs with strong, curved claws for gripping branches. Wide, rough pads on their feet give them sure footing on slippery limbs.

Scientists think that, over many generations, some kangaroos may have taken to the trees to escape enemies and to look for food. High in their leafy home, tree kangaroos move about at night, feeding on leaves and fruit. If startled, they leap to the forest floor, crashing through branches and landing with a loud thump.

The smallest kangaroos, called rat kangaroos, live on the floor of both the rain forests and the woodlands. About the size of small rabbits, they hop around at night scratching for insects and for seeds and other plant material to eat. They sleep during the day, hidden in shallow grass nests.

Another forest-dweller, the wombat, also stays out of sight during most of the day. This heavy-set animal weighs about 60 pounds (27 kg). Too large to hide in clumps of grass, the wombat digs an underground burrow. At night, it leaves its burrow to feed on grasses, roots, and bark. If it senses danger, it hurries back underground.

Rat kangaroos called brush-tailed bettongs touch noses (below). Like other members of the kangaroo family, bettongs hop on long back feet. They use their front paws to scratch plants, including fungi, out of the ground.

Like a fire fighter sliding down a pole, a Lumholtz's tree kangaroo scoots down a tree trunk (above). If it needs a faster getaway, it may leap to the ground, which may be as far as 50 feet (15 m) down.

A baby on her back, a brush-tailed possum makes her way along a log. A young brush-tailed possum spends its first five months in its mother's pouch. When it grows strong enough to leave the pouch, it rides on her back, clinging tightly with its tiny claws. Mother and young stay together for several months.

JEN AND DES BARTLETT

Pygmy possums cling to a banksia blossom (below). These mouse-like possums dip their bristle-tipped tongues into flowers to gather pollen, nectar, and insects. They use their long tails as extra hands as they climb.

KATHIE ATKINSON

Crouched on a branch, a greater glider (left) rests between leaps. Loose skin bunches along the animal's sides. When the glider is in the air, the skin acts as wing flaps.

An airborne sugar glider steers with its fluffy tail (above). This animal may travel 150 feet (46 m) in one leap. When it nears a tree, it draws in its hind legs, pulls its body upright, and lands on all fours.

Pushing off from a tree branch with its hind legs, a sugar glider launches its body into the air. Spreading both front and hind legs wide, it stretches out flaps of skin that catch the air the way wings do. It may travel half the length of a football field before landing on another tree.

This furry acrobat is a surprising sight. One witness described it this way: "It's as if the animal can suddenly turn its body into a piece of cloth." The glider's ability helps it get around in woodlands, where trees are spaced more widely apart.

Not many people see these daredevil members of the possum family, however. Like all possums, gliders move about at night. After dark, they leave their nests in tree hollows and take to the air. With graceful swooping dives, they move from tree to tree looking for leaves, fruit, sap, and insects to eat. They steer by moving their bushy tails and by changing the angle of their skin flaps. As they near their target tree, they pull in their legs. Then they

grab the trunk with their sharp claws. After they land, the loose skin folds out of the way.

Gliders vary in length from only inches to a few feet. The tiny feather-tailed glider is the smallest. About the size of a mouse, this glider gets its name from the feathery fringes of hair on the sides of its tail. The greater glider—the largest of the gliders—grows slightly bigger than a house cat. It makes long, silent glides, landing with a plop on a tree trunk. The sugar glider has few enemies. It moves noisily among the leaves. Its name reflects its taste for sweet foods such as fruit, sap, and flowers. The sugar glider also eats insects.

Besides steering, a glider's tail has another use, too. Some gliders carry masses of leaves and other nesting material in their curled-up tails.

Some gliders live in small groups. Several generations may share a nest in a tree hollow. A female glider carries her tiny young in a pouch. Later, they glide with her, clinging tightly to her back.

63

TOM AND PAM GARDNER/AUSTRALASIAN NATURE TRANSPARENCIES

Inside a courtship structure, a female satin bowerbird watches a male perform his courtship display. The glossy blue-black male built the twig structure—called a bower—to attract the olive-green female. He decorated the bower with bits of colored material. The birds will mate within the bower. Afterward, the female will move to a nearby wooded area and build a simple nest of twigs. There, she usually lays two eggs, and raises the chicks alone.

In the daytime, while many marsupials are asleep, both the rain forests and the woodlands brighten with the flashing colors and musical calls of birds. Birds in great variety—big and small, bold and shy—find the rain forest a good spot to feed, to stake out territories, and to find mates.

Some of the most elaborate courting is carried on by the male bowerbird. To attract a mate, the bowerbird carefully arranges twigs into a courtship structure called a bower. Then he decorates his bower with things he collects—bits of flowers, snail shells, and feathers. The bowerbird may add odds and ends such as clothespins or bottle caps. Some birds choose mostly blue and yellow objects to arrange around their bowers. Others pick mostly green. Some kinds of bowerbirds paint the inside walls of their bowers. They smear a mixture of crushed berries, dirt, and saliva onto the twigs with their beaks.

Bowers vary in size and shape. Some birds build large twig huts. Others arrange sticks into a long narrow avenue. Finished bowers look so impressive that early explorers who came upon them in the forest thought humans had built them.

A bower becomes a stage for the male's courtship displays. With a female as his audience, the male performs a lively dance, flashing his feathers as he hops and struts. Some males add to their display a loud song that often expertly mimics other birds and even galloping horses and barking dogs. After mating, each bird goes its own way. The female raises the young alone.

Another unusual bird, the male lyrebird, has sixteen silvery tail feathers almost 2 feet (2/3 m) long that he uses during courtship. When spread out, these feathers form a pattern that resembles a harp-like instrument called a lyre. Before performing his courtship display, the lyrebird scratches together a

C. A. HENLEY/AUSTRALASIAN NATURE TRANSPARENCIES (OPPOSITE)

Rainbow lorikeets add color to bare branches. At dawn and in the late afternoon, they will flock to feeding areas, screeching and chattering. Lorikeets sip the juices of flowers and fruits.

Australian cassowary chicks feed under the watchful eye of their father (above). Male cassowaries care for the young for about nine months after they hatch. As adults, these chicks will have the colorful skin and bony headpiece of their parents. Cassowaries cannot fly, but they run fast.

mound of earth. When a female approaches, he stands on the mound and sings. His courtship consists of a collection of loud mimicked bird calls and other noises. As he sings, he moves about in a hopping dance and fans his tail feathers over his head.

Many birds of the Australian forests gather in colorful, noisy flocks. At dawn and in the late afternoon, rainbow and scaly-breasted lorikeets fly to flowering trees and feed on nectar—plant juices—and pollen. Lorikeets, brightly colored members of the parrot family, chatter and screech as they feed. These birds, which have orange-red, blue, green, and yellow feathers, climb easily up and down branches. They dip their bristly tongues into flowers to collect nectar and pollen. At sunset, the birds leave the feeding area and roost in tall trees nearby.

When a bird known as the kookaburra (KOOK-uh-burr-uh) calls, most people think the call sounds like a human laugh. Hearing the strange sound, early settlers wondered if laughing spirits hid in the woodlands. The kookaburra's call warns other birds to stay away from its territory. When a kookaburra hunts, it sits silently, listening and watching for signs of prey on the ground below. If it detects a lizard, a snake, or some other small animal, it swoops down and catches it in its large, strong beak.

Not all birds are easy to detect. The tawny frogmouth, for example, seems almost to vanish when it sits quietly on a branch. This bird's mottled feathers resemble bark. Sitting perfectly still, frogmouths are well camouflaged from enemies—and from prey.

One of the forest's shyest birds is also its largest. The cassowary (KASS-uh-ware-ee) stands about 5 feet ($1\frac{1}{2}$ m) tall. The cassowary can't fly, but it doesn't need to. Its size and the thick vegetation of its home protect it from enemies. When startled, a cassowary lowers its big body and runs swiftly into the underbrush. Should an enemy corner it, the cassowary kicks with its strong legs, slashing out with the daggerlike nail on the inner toe of each foot.

Displaying for a nearby female, a superb lyrebird (left) spreads his tail feathers in a graceful arch over his head. During his performance, he does a hopping dance and sings loudly, sometimes mimicking the calls of other birds. The superb lyrebird uses a mound in a clearing as his stage.

Ignoring its tiny attacker, a laughing kookaburra keeps its perch (above). Kookaburras usually hunt small lizards, snakes, and insects. Occasionally they feed on newly hatched nestlings. To protect its young, the smaller bird, called a willie wagtail, tries to drive the laughing kookaburra away.

Bird or branch? The coloring of this pair of tawny frogmouths makes it difficult to tell. During the day, these birds roost quietly in trees. With heads turned upward and eyes partly closed, they blend with the branches. At night, they fly to the ground to hunt insects and spiders.

If you asked Australians to name their favorite animal, many would choose the koala. This cuddly looking animal resembles a teddy bear. The koala has a roly-poly body, furry ears, and a smooth, leathery nose.

Though they resemble bears and sometimes are called bears, koalas are not bears. They are marsupials. They climb easily, clinging to branches with their sharp-clawed toes. In trees, food is always within reach. Koalas eat mostly the leaves of the eucalyptus tree. In the evening, they move among the branches, stripping off leaves and young shoots. A koala eats about 2½ pounds (1 kg) of eucalyptus leaves a day. A strong-smelling oil in the leaves gives the koala a distinct odor that some kinds of cough drops have.

During the day, koalas sleep curled up high in the treetops—often in a tree fork. A koala may spend as much as 20 hours a day resting. Usually, a koala perches alone in a tree. During mating season, the male koala warns rivals away from certain trees that he claims as his home range. The male koala calls with a loud grunting sound.

Female koalas give birth usually to one youngster a year. The young koala stays with its mother throughout the year, first in her pouch, then riding on her back or following close by. After that, it goes off to live on its own.

At one time, koalas nearly died out. Disease and the destruction of their habitat killed many koalas. Hunters killed millions more for their soft fur. Laws now protect koalas from hunters, but the continuing

High in a eucalyptus tree, a koala relaxes (left). With few enemies to fear, koalas lead quiet lives in the treetops. In the evening, they may climb to the ground and walk to another tree.

JEN AND DES BARTLETT (ALL)

Young look-alike hitches a ride on its mother's back (above). Before it grows large enough to travel this way, the young koala spends six months in its mother's pouch. There, the thimble-size newborn stays safe and protected. After growing for several months, it begins to eat leaves.

With her young safe in her lap, a female koala reaches for food. Picky eaters, these furry animals feed on the leaves of eucalyptus trees. Their leafy diet also provides them with most of the moisture they need.

destruction of their habitat is still a problem.

Another Australian animal, the red-necked wallaby, lives in the woodlands and nearby open areas. This medium-size member of the kangaroo family is named for the reddish fur on the back of its neck and shoulders. During the day, it takes cover among the trees, resting in patches of thick vegetation. In the late afternoon, it moves toward an open area to feed on grasses and herbs.

Although red-necked wallabies usually live alone, they sometimes gather in groups to feed. Before dark, the wallabies stay close to the forest edge. If danger threatens, they scramble back to the safety of the trees. Powered by their muscular hind legs, they spring easily over logs, bushes, and stumps in their path. The animals use their tails for balance as they leap.

In the summer, blossoming flowers attract an acrobatic visitor to the forest. People call it the flying fox, but it's really a fruit bat—one of the largest bats in the world. Its unusually shaped head gives the flying fox its name. Large eyes and a sharply pointed snout make it look like a fox. In the air, it looks like a giant bird. Its spread wings measure more than 4 feet (1 m) across.

Flying foxes roost in forests in gathering places

H**ead outstretched, a red-necked wallaby leaps over a fallen tree. When the wallaby is in a hurry, its front legs never touch the ground. The animal** bounces through the forest on powerful hind legs, leaping over obstacles along the way. Its outstretched tail helps the wallaby keep its balance as it travels.

KATHIE ATKINSON (BOTH)

Hanging by a clawed foot, a flying fox dozes. Hundreds of large bats like this one may roost in a tree. Before sleeping, they wrap their wings around their bodies like cloaks.

Fanning the air with one wing helps a flying fox cool itself. These bats have claws on their feet and at the edges of their wings. As they move among the trees, feeding on fruit and flowers, they swing along the branches by hooking onto them with their claws.

called camps. One camp may include tens of thousands of these bats.

Flying foxes eat fruits and flowers. During the day, the animals hang upside down from branches by the hooked claws on their feet. At dusk, they fly to blossoms and to fruit trees, sometimes forming long columns in the sky. They use their keen sense of smell to locate flowers and ripe fruit. To feed, flying foxes mash soft fruits and blossoms between their tongues and the roofs of their mouths. They swallow the juices and spit out most of the rest.

Female flying foxes give birth to a single youngster soon after the camps form. At first, the female carries her baby along with her. It firmly grasps her body underneath when she flies and hangs onto her back when she climbs.

When it is older, she leaves it at the camp, feeding it when she returns. Each young bat has an individual odor that enables its mother to recognize it. The young begin to fly at about two months. Soon after, they can find food on their own.

In the fall, small groups of bats begin leaving the camp, scattering widely to other areas where they spend the winter. They will return the next summer. Sometimes they form their camps in the same area year after year.

71

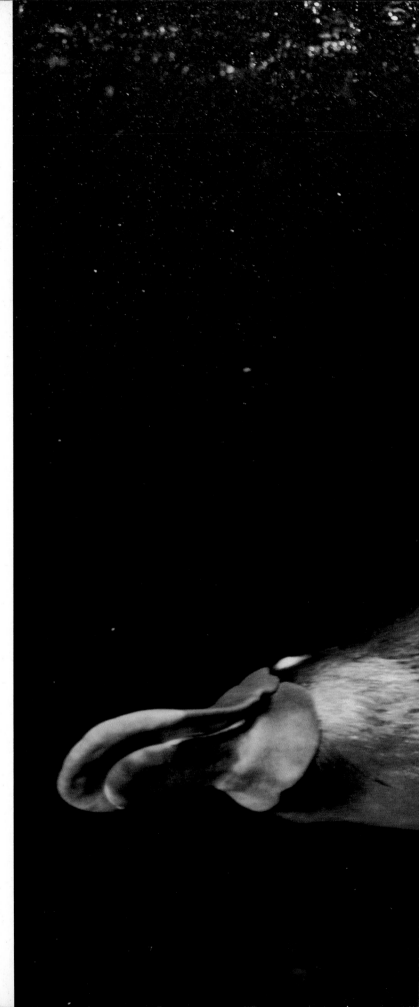

A quiet riverbank conceals the home of one of the world's most unusual animals—the platypus. This timid but curious mammal digs its burrow just above the water's edge.

When scientists first heard about the platypus, they thought it must be a fake. People who had seen this strange animal said it had a bill and webbed feet like a duck's, fur like an otter's, and a tail like a beaver's. Stranger still, they found later that its young hatched from eggs!

Scientists discovered that the unusual animal is one of only two kinds of egg-laying mammals in the world. The other is the echidna.

With its odd combination of features, the platypus is equally at home on land or in the water. Although it sleeps in a burrow in the bank of a stream or a lake, it feeds in the water. It spends several hours a day diving for food. The platypus swims along the bottom, propelled by its webbed front feet. It sweeps its sensitive muzzle from side to side to detect the insects, small shellfish, and other water creatures on which it feeds. After about a minute, the platypus comes to the surface, its catch stored in pouches in its cheeks. Floating with feet spread, it chews the food it has gathered. Instead of teeth, an adult platypus has hard grinding pads with shearing ridges. It removes the shell and other hard parts of

Swimming gracefully, a platypus paddles with its webbed front feet. Its hind feet and beaverlike tail trail behind, helping it to steer. Underwater, its eyelids close and folds of skin cover its eyes and ears. It uses its sensitive, skin-covered muzzle to search out prey on the stream bottom. A sleek outer layer of fur keeps the thick, woolly undercoat dry—even after hours in the water.

the prey and crushes its meal between the pads.

On land, the webbing of the platypus's forefeet folds up into the animal's palms. This frees its paws for walking and for digging. The platypus digs its burrow just above the water's edge. After loosening the earth with its nails, it packs it down with its body and tail.

Before the female platypus lays her eggs, she digs a separate nesting burrow. She lines a small chamber at the end with plant material she has gathered from the water and its bank. She lays one, two, or three leathery eggs, then tucks them between her folded tail and her belly to keep them warm. In about ten days, the platypuses hatch. The young, bean-size and hairless, feed on milk that oozes from pores on the mother's belly.

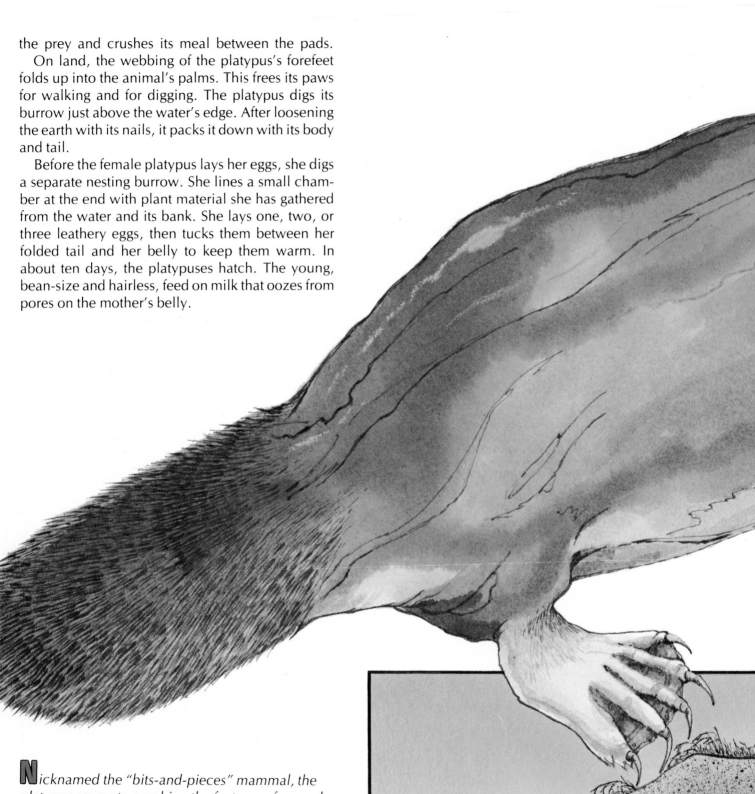

Nicknamed the "bits-and-pieces" mammal, the platypus seems to combine the features of several different animals. In this drawing, the platypus's feet have been tilted slightly outward. The artist adjusted them so that you can get a good look at the webbing between its nails.

DOROTHY MICHELLE NOVICK

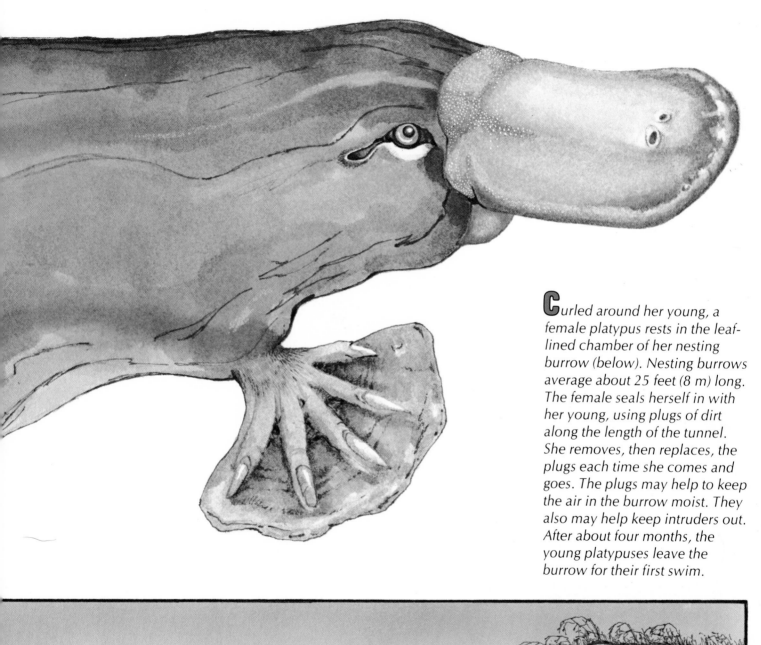

Curled around her young, a female platypus rests in the leaf-lined chamber of her nesting burrow (below). Nesting burrows average about 25 feet (8 m) long. The female seals herself in with her young, using plugs of dirt along the length of the tunnel. She removes, then replaces, the plugs each time she comes and goes. The plugs may help to keep the air in the burrow moist. They also may help keep intruders out. After about four months, the young platypuses leave the burrow for their first swim.

On stage at the Taronga Zoo Theatre, an Australian fur seal and her pup do tricks for a crowd (left). Seal trainers explain how the seals live in the wild. At this zoo, overlooking Sydney's harbor, visitors get a close look at many Australian animals.

A Goodfellow's tree kangaroo from Papua New Guinea accepts a gardenia from attendant Carol Palmer (above). Most of the zoo animals live in surroundings that match their homes in the wild as closely as possible. Tree kangaroos spend much of their time in trees.

If you wanted to see all the strange and wonderful creatures of Australia, you would have to travel from rocky beaches to wilderness grasslands to tangled rain forests. Even if you made such a journey, you might see only a few of the animals that live in Australia. Many Australian animals are timid, and move about mostly at night. For instance, the tiny Leadbeater's possum hides so expertly that, for more than 50 years, scientists thought it was extinct. It was finally rediscovered living in thick woodlands in southeastern Australia.

At the Taronga Zoo, in Sydney, people can see a Leadbeater's possum, along with many other animals from Australia—and from other parts of the world as well. Many are threatened species seldom spotted in the wild. In the zoo, the animals live in surroundings much like their natural homes. Instead of living in cages, most roam open areas.

At a bird exhibit, visitors walk through a tropical garden and feel as though they had entered a rain forest. More than 20 varieties of birds live in this mini-jungle. Visitors might spot the colorful feathers of rainbow lorikeets in the tall trees. Lyrebirds spread their long, graceful tail feathers as they move about in the undergrowth.

Another exhibit turns day into night. Special lighting provides a moonlit setting for animals that normally move about after dark. Visitors can watch the spotted cuscus, the grey-headed flying fox, the sugar glider, and the common wombat. In another part of the zoo, they can see the timid platypus as it comes out of its burrow to eat.

Some of the zoo's most popular residents—the koalas—climb about undisturbed in tall trees, while visitors watch from a ramp. To provide the koalas with the leafy diet they need, the zoo has its own forest of thousands of eucalyptus trees.

Young visitors get an even closer look at some of

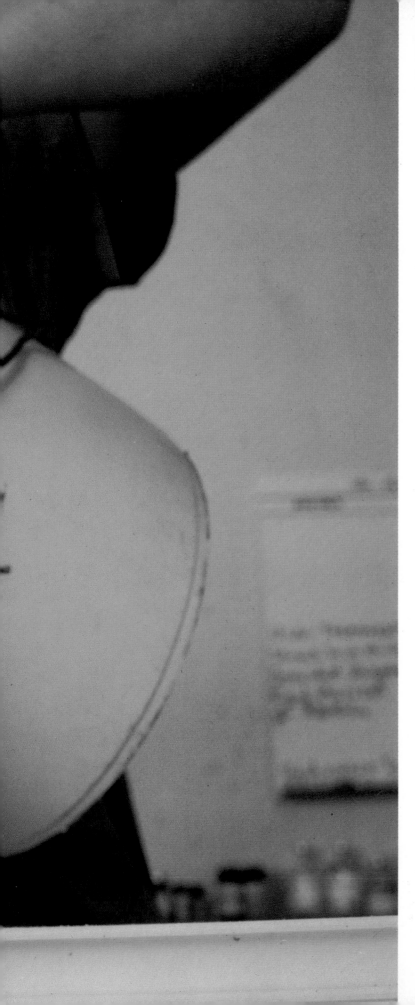

Ding, a five-month-old flying fox, clings to Meena Chandran, 10, of Sydney (above). "I also held a wombat and a ring-tailed possum," says Meena.

A wombat gets a bath from zookeeper Andrew Crebbin (left). At the zoo clinic, animals have regular checkups to keep them healthy. The clinic also treats injured, sick, or orphaned native animals.

the animals. At an education center, schoolchildren carefully handle wombats, snakes, turtles, possums, and bats. The zoo staff tells them about each animal's special traits. "At first I was scared to hold a fruit bat," says Meena Chandran, 10, of Sydney. "But when I did, it hugged me. The people at the zoo said it has very sensitive wings and likes to eat sweet things."

The zoo staff hopes that getting to know such animals as the fruit bat will encourage people to protect wildlife. "These animals are ambassadors for their wild relatives," says one staff member. "When people see an animal here, they learn about how that animal lives in the wild."

79

4. Tasmania

A black currawong (KUR-uh-wong), left, and a Bennett's wallaby share a meadow in Tasmania. Once part of the mainland, Tasmania was cut off some 11,000 years ago. Today, some species extinct on the mainland survive here.

81

Forests and mountains cover large areas of Tasmania (red), Australia's southernmost state. Here, temperatures generally remain cooler than on the mainland.

What's a Tasmanian devil? People all over the world recognize it as the villain in Bugs Bunny cartoons. But there is a living animal called a Tasmanian devil. It's a marsupial found only in the state of Tasmania, an island off the southeastern tip of the Australian mainland. Partly because of the cartoon's popularity, the real devil has become one of the most famous animals in Tasmania.

Even most Tasmanians know little about Tasmanian devils. To find out more about their habits and their behavior, David Pemberton, a graduate zoology student at the University of Tasmania, in Hobart, began a two-year field study of these marsupials. Assisted by his wife, Heather, he works out of a cabin in Mount William National Park, a wild area in the northeastern corner of the island.

"This park was set up as a preserve for the forester kangaroo, the big roo that has been killed off in most of Tasmania," says David. "Here it's fairly common. The park is also filled with other wildlife—devils, wallabies, pademelons (PAD-dee-mel-unz), even rarely seen tiger quolls (KWALZ)."

Is the Tasmanian devil really as devilish as the cartoons suggest? According to David, the island's early settlers gave the devil its bad name before they had seen it. They didn't like its fearsome screech. Some Tasmanians call the devil Australia's ugliest marsupial. About the size of a pug dog, it looks like a small, heavyset bear. It has a big head, short, pointed ears, and a stiff, carrot-shaped tail. Its black fur is usually spotted with a patch of white at the neck—"beautiful markings," David says.

Although many farmers consider the devil a killer of livestock, David is trying to show that the animal doesn't deserve that reputation. The devil hunts by smell and eats mostly the remains of dead animals.

In a rocky section of Mount William National Park, David Pemberton (left) looks for dens of Tasmanian devils. David, a graduate student at the University of Tasmania, is studying these marsupials in the wild. Once found on the mainland, they now survive only in Tasmania.

A disturbed Tasmanian devil snarls (right) after being released from a trap. "Typical behavior," says David. "The animal turned to a threat posture and froze. Devils will stay that way until you go away." Devils look and sound fierce, but they are not known as hunters. They seem to eat mostly the remains of dead animals.

PENNY TWEEDIE (BOTH)

83

Occasionally, however, it will attack weak lambs and penned poultry.

David knows a lot about Tasmanian devils because he often meets these animals face-to-face in the wild. "Four times a year, I set 50 cage traps over an 8-day period," he says. "We catch between 5 and 20 devils a day. I measure them and record their age, sex, markings, and condition. Then I release them and reset the traps."

When he isn't trapping, David tracks devils to their dens to observe them. While he was making the field trip shown on these pages, he was awaiting delivery of a radio tracking unit. This device fits on a special transmitter collar. David will place collars on some devils he traps. The transmitters give off signals that a receiver picks up. The signals make it easier to follow the animals. In the meantime, David follows Tasmanian devil footprints. He likes his work so much that he and Heather have raised a devil as a pet. It even sleeps on their bed.

David checks the markings of a devil (above) taken from one of his traps. His injured arm resulted from a motorbike spill, not from a bite. "I've trapped hundreds of devils," he says, "and no bites yet."

Sitting on a trap, David controls a devil while Heather, his wife, measures it (right). "Putting it in a sack makes for easier handling," he says. "It's also easier when two people work together."

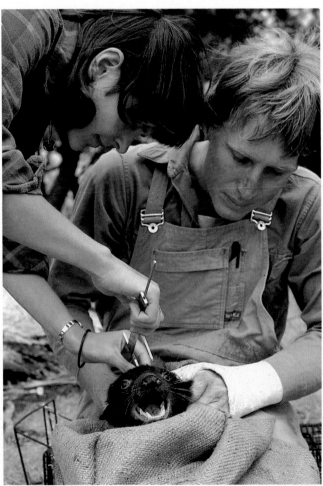

84

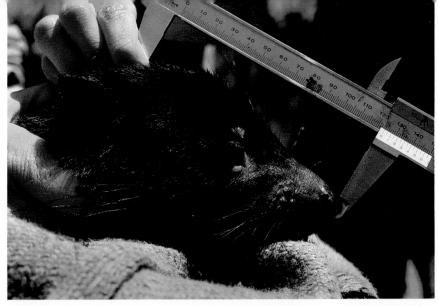

A measuring device called calipers shows that this young devil's head is about 4¾ inches (12 cm) long (left). The Pembertons also check its teeth. This helps them estimate its age.

After tattooing an identification number on its ear, David releases a devil (below). Devils usually stay in remote regions, but they may wander near urban areas.

nimals brought from other lands, such as the dingo and the fox, helped destroy much of Australia's native wildlife. But these two predators never reached Tasmania. Neither did the large numbers of settlers that disturbed the woodland habitats of many mainland species. So a number of animals either extinct or reduced in number on the mainland still thrive in the island-state.

The Tasmanian bettong (BEH-tong), for example, survives only in Tasmania. This animal, a kind of rat kangaroo, lives on grassy plains. It builds a nest of grass, carrying the grass wrapped in its tail.

Few people on the mainland ever catch a glimpse of the tiger quoll, also known as the tiger cat. But quite a few of these animals survive in Tasmania. In spite of its name, the quoll is neither a tiger nor a cat, but a marsupial. Like a cat, however, it climbs trees easily and hunts skillfully.

Many other creatures—lizards, flightless birds, potoroos (poh-duh-RUHZ), pademelons, wombats (WAHM-batz), bandicoots—also live in Tasmania. But the animal receiving the most attention today may be extinct in both places—a large meat-eating marsupial called the thylacine (THY-luh-seen).

The blotched blue-tongued lizard (above) belongs to a family of lizards called skinks. This lizard is common in the cool woodlands of Tasmania. When frightened, it sticks out its blue tongue, puffs up its body, and hisses. But it's harmless.

A Tasmanian bettong rests in its nest (above). The bettong builds a mound-shaped nest of grass and other materials. It carries the materials to the nesting site wrapped in its tail.

Ready for a fight, a Tasmanian tiger quoll shows its teeth (right). Quolls climb trees as cats do, hunting birds and raiding nests. They live mostly in forests. About 4 feet (1 $\frac{1}{4}$ m) long, from nose to tip of tail, adult quolls sometimes attack small wallabies and raid poultry houses.

In Tasmania's cool climate, a pademelon feeds in the daylight (below). It nibbles on grasses and herbs, but never travels far from the shelter of thickets. In mountainous areas, it digs through snow with its forepaws to uncover vegetation. Like rabbits, pademelons thump the ground with their hind feet, perhaps to send signals to other pademelons.

Until recently, when you asked a scientist if the thylacine still stalked the wilds of Tasmania, the answer was "Probably not." Now it's "Maybe." The thylacine, also called the Tasmanian tiger or Tasmanian wolf, once lived throughout Australia and on the island of New Guinea. Several thousand years ago, however, its range shrank to Tasmania.

When farmers settled in Tasmania, they cleared much of the land where the thylacines lived. To survive, the animals began feeding on sheep and poultry. The farmers reacted by killing thylacines in great numbers. This, plus an outbreak of disease about 1910, brought the thylacine close to extinction. The last known thylacine died in a Tasmanian zoo in the 1930s.

Since then, hundreds of people have reported seeing thylacines, but no one has presented proof. In 1982, however, a field biologist in northwestern Tasmania reported a sighting, and now scientists have begun an all-out search for the animal. And an American has offered a $100,000 reward for proof that the thylacine still exists.

If thylacines still roam the woodlands of Tasmania, here's what they look like. A yawning male reveals wide-gaping jaws. These enable him to seize large prey by the throat. Marsupials about the size of German shepherd dogs, thylacines look somewhat like wolves. They can't run very fast. They rely on a steady jogging pace to wear down their prey—kangaroos, wallabies, and small mammals. The female thylacine, slightly smaller than her 5½-foot-long (1¾-m) mate, has a backward-facing pouch, not visible here. It protects her young from branches as she moves through the brush.

FRANK FRETZ (ART)

5. Helping Animals Survive

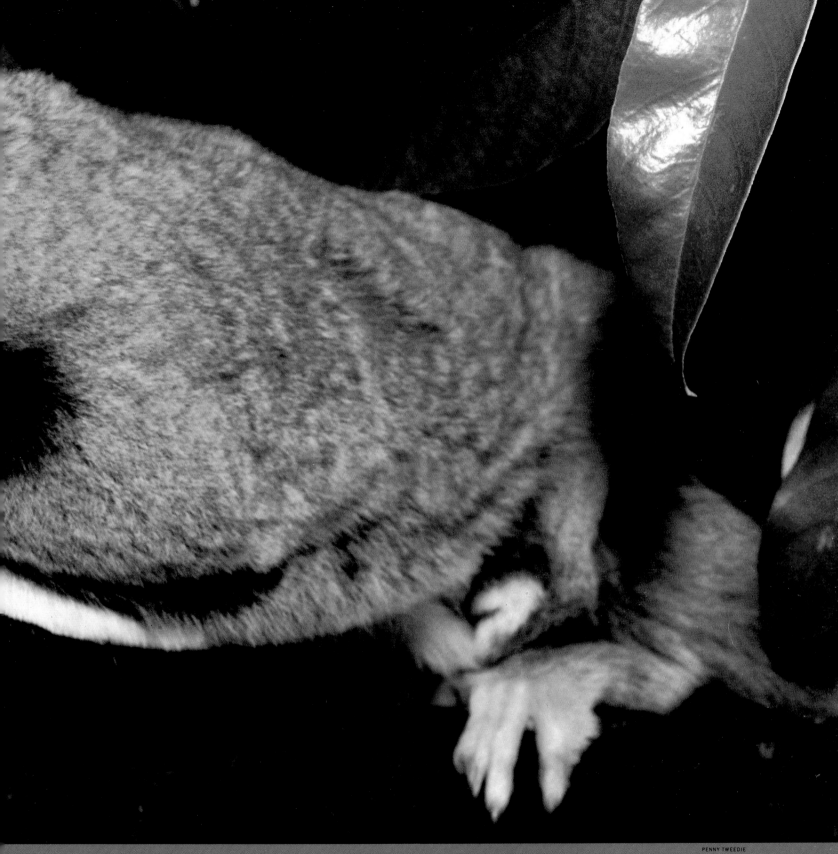

Disturbed by a light, a squirrel glider crouches on a branch at a research center near Townsville, in Queensland.

Here, and at other research centers across Australia, scientists are studying animals to help ensure their future.

Unusual . . . fascinating . . . unique. . . . These are all words you might use to describe Australian animals. In some cases, however, you would have to add the word endangered. In Australia, as in other countries, many animals are disappearing from places where they have always lived. Some have already become extinct. Others need help right away to survive. To protect endangered animals—and to prevent others from becoming endangered—scientists are trying to learn more about them. How many animals remain? Where do they live? How do they behave? What do they need to survive?

At the Northern Regional Centre of the Queensland National Parks and Wildlife Service, near Townsville, scientists are trying to provide answers to these and other important questions. They do this partly by studying an animal in the wild, where they can see how it acts in its natural habitat. But many Australian animals are too small to track easily. Others hide. Still others move about mostly at night, and are difficult to study out-of-doors. So scientists capture some animals and care for them at the Centre. There they can observe the animals up close, over a long period of time.

One animal under study at the Centre is the squirrel glider, a possum that swoops from tree to tree with the help of a flap of loose skin stretching between its wrists and its ankles. Although not endangered, the squirrel glider lives only in small patches of forest in eastern Australia. People often confuse

PENNY TWEEDIE (BOTH)

A squirrel glider perches atop a branch at the Northern Regional Centre (left). You can see the edge of the skin that stretches between the glider's wrist and ankle. The animal spreads four legs to glide from tree to tree. The box behind the glider serves as a sleeping den for the animal during the day.

In a forest near Townsville, Andrew Haffenden, a research technician, inspects a squirrel glider that he has just caught (right). He will take the glider back to the Centre for study. Scientists want to find out how many squirrel gliders remain and where they live.

this glider with the sugar glider, a close relative. By studying squirrel gliders at the Centre, scientists and other field staff can better identify them and find out how many squirrel gliders there really are.

Staff members at the Centre also are studying the brolga (BROHL-guh), a crane native to Australia. This tall, shiny gray bird breeds mainly in the coastal swamps of eastern and northern Australia and in inland freshwater swamps. In the south where humans have drained and filled in many of these swamps, brolgas have all but disappeared. Scientists at the Centre have been studying the cranes for more than 25 years. They have recorded how the birds feed, mate, nest, and raise their young. In the wild, the scientists have counted the numbers of birds, followed their movements, and observed their behavior at different times of the year. "We

now have a good understanding of the bird," says Andrew Haffenden, a research technician at the Centre. "We are on our way to understanding its needs."

The eastern sarus (SAH-rus) crane—a close relative of the brolga—also concerns scientists at the Centre. This endangered bird once lived in much of southeast Asia. Now it is known to exist only in northern Australia. The staff at the Centre is trying to find out exactly how many eastern sarus cranes there are, and how they get along with the brolgas, which share the same area. Brolgas and eastern sarus cranes are so closely related that they can mate and produce fertile offspring. As a result, some scientists believe that continued breeding between brolga and sarus cranes might produce an entirely new species—the "sarolga."

ANIMALS ANIMALS/FRITZ PRENZEL

Searching for food, a brolga wades through a swamp in eastern Australia (above). Draining swamps for pastures and farmland threatens the survival of brolgas in some areas.

Inside a large enclosure at the Centre, zoologist Gavin Blackman holds a brolga (below). Andrew prepares to slip a hood over its head. The hood will calm the bird while Andrew takes its measurements and checks the growth pattern of its feathers. "This helps us understand how the bird grows," he says.

94

Five days old, an eastern sarus crane accepts a handout from Andrew. The chick hatched at the Centre. The staff will feed it until it can eat by itself. Eastern sarus cranes once lived and bred all over southeast Asia. Few, if any, are now found outside of northern Australia. Scientists are studying the relationship between this endangered bird and the brolga, its close relative.

G. B. BAKER/AUSTRALASIAN NATURE TRANSPARENCIES

In studying endangered animals, scientists try to find out why the animals are disappearing. Endangered animals face many problems. The most common one, however, is that humans and other animals are changing, destroying, or taking over the habitats of these animals.

Some remote areas of Australia are home to the ghost bat. This large bat is the only Australian member of a family of meat-eating bats called false vampires. Easily disturbed, ghost bats roost, feed, and raise their young in caves, in spaces between rocks, and in abandoned mine shafts. Scientists fear that, in some areas, limestone miners working near these sites may threaten the very survival of these bats.

Other animals face growing competition for food and space. When Europeans settled in Australia, some brought along foxes, rabbits, and other animals not found in Australia. The introduced animals spread quickly. One Australian animal that suffered as a result is the bilby, or rabbit-eared bandicoot. It digs burrows. Foxes preyed upon the bilby. Rabbits took over its burrows. The once-common bilby became rare. Competition from rabbits may also have caused a drastic decline in the number of burrowing bettongs, the only kangaroos that live year-round in burrows. Scientists are working to increase the

Flapping wings that measure about 2 feet (1/2 m) across, a ghost bat carries a freshly caught mouse (left). The only meat-eating bat in Australia, this big bat feeds on large insects, lizards, frogs, birds, and small mammals.

During the day, ghost bats roost on the wall of an abandoned building (above). They also may hide in caves and in empty mine shafts. People working near these sites may disturb the ghost bats and threaten their survival.

A tail about twice as long as its head and body combined helps a long-tailed dunnart keep its balance in its rocky desert habitat (right). The tail measures 8 inches (20 cm) long. Until 1981, scientists had found the remains of just four of these marsupials. Then nine dunnarts were captured. Now experts can study these rare animals and learn how to protect them.

number of these marsupials, which are also known as Lesueur's rat kangaroos.

Clearing land for agriculture has destroyed the homes of such animals as the numbat. This small, bushy-tailed animal lives in the woodlands of southwestern Australia. The woodlands support large colonies of termites—the numbat's usual food. In a single day, a numbat may eat several thousand termites. Cutting down these woodlands leaves the numbat without food or shelter.

To help solve these problems, the state governments of Australia have passed laws prohibiting people from killing or collecting endangered animals. They have set aside protected areas where animals such as the bridled nail-tailed wallaby, once thought to be extinct, can roam undisturbed. At research centers, scientists are helping such animals as the bilby to reproduce. And they are returning some of the young to areas where these animals once lived in the wild.

MICHAEL AND IRENE MORCOMBE

© JEAN-PAUL FERRERO

Only kangaroo that lives year-round in a burrow, the once-common burrowing bettong (above) survives on just four islands. Experts say that it may be extinct on the mainland.

A numbat laps termites from a fallen tree with its long, thin tongue (left). Numbats live only in woodlands that support large colonies of termites. In recent years, fewer and fewer numbats have been sighted.

With its long snout, a bilby sniffs its surroundings in an outdoor enclosure at a research center in central Australia (left). Scientists there have raised more than 30 bilbies and returned them to the wild.

A bridle-like shoulder stripe and a tiny spike at the tip of its tail give the bridled nail-tailed wallaby its name (right). For more than 30 years, scientists feared that this animal was extinct. Then, in the early 1970s, they found a small group living in Queensland.

PENNY TWEEDIE

On Dirk Hartog Island, off the coast of Western Australia, Dr. Robert I. T. Prince releases a banded hare wallaby (above). This kind of wallaby survives naturally on only two western islands. Scientists hope they will reestablish a colony here.

Close friends. Seven-year-old Ben Tweedie and a koala share a hug at a wildlife park in New South Wales (right). They have reason for celebrating. About 50 years ago, koalas almost died out. Today, because concerned people are helping the koalas, their numbers are growing again.

You may wonder: How successful have these efforts to protect Australia's wildlife really been? In some cases, it's too soon to tell. In others, results are beginning to come in.

Take the case of banded hare wallabies. These animals, named for the banded patterns on their backs, once lived on the southwestern Australian mainland and on a few islands off that coast. By the late 1920s, they had vanished from everywhere except two islands. In 1973, a fire on one island destroyed many plants that provided food and shelter for the animals. Scientists collected 11 of the surviving wallabies and moved them to small enclosures on nearby Dirk Hartog Island, where this kind of wallaby once lived. By 1976, the colony had grown to 35 animals. The following year, scientists released some of the wallabies on the island.

Researchers have since returned to the island to check on the wallabies. They found that some animals had died during a drought in 1980. Wandering cats may have killed others. But scientists continue to help the wallabies. They hope that in time the animals will once again establish a permanent home on the island.

As wallaby-watchers await the outcome of this project, one of Australia's most popular animals—the koala—is making a comeback. Until the early 1900s, millions of koalas climbed about their woodland habitat. Then hunters began killing koalas for their soft fur. In 1924 alone, traders shipped more than two million koala skins out of the country. Meanwhile, people were clearing more and more of the koalas' habitat to make room for farms. Disease killed other koalas. In some areas, koalas were nearly wiped out.

State governments took action. They passed strict laws to help protect koalas. They set up preserves where the animals could live undisturbed in the treetops. With this help, the numbers of koalas began to increase. Although koalas may never thrive as they did in the past, these animals are—at least for now—out of danger.

Index

Additional Reading

Readers may want to check the *National Geographic* or WORLD *Index* in a school or a public library for related articles and to refer to the following books. ("A" indicates a book for readers at the adult level.)

Bergamini, David, and the Editors of Time-Life Books, *The Land and Wildlife of Australasia,* Time-Life Books, 1980. Breeden, Stanley and Kay, *Australia's North,* W. Collins, 1980 (A). Breeden, Stanley and Kay, *Life of the Kangaroo,* Taplinger Publishing, 1967 (A). Coerr, Eleanor, *Biography of a Kangaroo,* G. P. Putnam's Sons, 1976. Ferrier, Lucy, *Diving the Great Barrier Reef,* Troll Associates, 1976. Havlicek, Karel, and Walter Stuart, *Koalas,* Wildlife Education, Ltd., 1983. *Kangaroos & Other Creatures from Down Under,* Time-Life Films, 1978. *Koalas and Kangaroos: Strange Animals of Australia,* National Geographic Society, 1981. Lavery, H. J., ed., *Exploration North: Australia's Wildlife from Desert to Reef,* Richmond Hill Press, 1978 (A). Lavine, Sigmund A., *Wonders of Marsupials,* Dodd, Mead, 1979. McGregor, Craig, *The Great Barrier Reef,* Time-Life Books, 1973. *National Geographic Book of Mammals,* Vols. 1 and 2, National Geographic Society, 1981. Rau, Margaret, *The Gray Kangaroo at Home,* Alfred A. Knopf, 1978. Simpson, Ken, and Nicholas Day, *Birds of Australia,* Tanager Books, 1984. Strahan, Ronald, ed., *Complete Book of Australian Mammals: The National Photographic Index of Australian Wildlife,* Merrimack, 1984 (A).

EDUCATIONAL CONSULTANTS

Larry R. Collins, National Zoological Park, Smithsonian Institution; Hugh J. Lavery, Queensland National Parks and Wildlife Service, *Chief Consultants*

Glenn O. Blough, LL.D., Emeritus Professor of Education, University of Maryland, *Educational Consultant*

Nicholas J. Long, Ph.D., *Consulting Psychologist*

Joan Myers, *Reading Consultant*

The Special Publications and School Services Division is also grateful to the individuals and institutions named or quoted within the text and to those cited here for their generous assistance:

Gerald Borgia, University of Maryland; Frank N. Carrick, University of Queensland; Darill Clements, Taronga Zoo; Bela Demeter, National Zoological Park, Smithsonian Institution; Scott Derrickson, National Zoological Park, Smithsonian Institution; Gary F. Hevel, Department of Entomology, Smithsonian Institution; Ken Johnson, Conservation Commission of the Northern Territory; Leslie S. Kaufman, New England Aquarium; Patricia Kay, Embassy of Australia; Rudie H. Kuiter, Museum of Victoria; Colin J. Limpus, Queensland National Parks and Wildlife Service; Philip K. Lundeberg, Division of Naval History, Smithsonian Institution; Carmi Penny, San Diego Zoo; David B. Rowley, University of Chicago; Ralph W. Schreiber, Los Angeles County Museum of Natural History; Kevin Siebert, Division of Mapping, Australia; Charles M. Wahle, University of Maryland; George E. Watson, Smithsonian Institution; Warren Webb, Division of Mapping, Australia.

Composition for AMAZING ANIMALS OF AUSTRALIA by National Geographic's Photographic Services, Carl M. Shrader, Director; Lawrence F. Ludwig, Assistant Director. Printed and bound by Holladay-Tyler Printing Corp., Rockville, Md. Color separations by the Lanman-Progressive Co., Washington, D. C.; Lincoln Graphics, Inc., Cherry Hill, N.J.; NEC, Inc., Nashville, Tenn. FAR-OUT FUN! printed by McCollum Press, Inc., Rockville, Md. *Classroom Activities* produced by Mazer Corp., Dayton, Ohio.

Library of Congress CIP Data

Main entry under title:

Amazing animals of Australia.

    (Books for world explorers)

    Bibliography: p.

    Includes index.

    SUMMARY: Describes the kangaroo, platypus, and other animals native to Australia and discusses their origin and adaptation to their environment.

    1. Zoology—Australia—Juvenile literature. [1. Zoology—Australia] I. Series.

QL338.A64   1985   599.0994   84-29558

ISBN 0-87044-515-4 (regular edition)

ISBN 0-87044-520-0 (library edition)

AMAZING ANIMALS OF AUSTRALIA

PUBLISHED BY
THE NATIONAL GEOGRAPHIC SOCIETY
WASHINGTON, D. C.

Gilbert M. Grosvenor, *President*
Melvin M. Payne, *Chairman of the Board*
Owen R. Anderson, *Executive Vice President*
Robert L. Breeden, *Vice President,
Publications and Educational Media*

PREPARED BY THE SPECIAL PUBLICATIONS
AND SCHOOL SERVICES DIVISION

Donald J. Crump, *Director*
Philip B. Silcott, *Associate Director*
William L. Allen, *Assistant Director*

BOOKS FOR WORLD EXPLORERS
Ralph Gray, *Editor*
Pat Robbins, *Managing Editor*
Ursula Perrin Vosseler, *Art Director*

STAFF FOR *AMAZING ANIMALS OF AUSTRALIA*
Margaret McKelway, *Managing Editor*
Thomas B. Powell III, *Picture Editor*
Louise Ponsford, *Designer*
Sharon L. Barry, James A. Cox, Robin Darcy Dennis, Theresa Knight McFadden, Catherine O'Neill, *Writers*
Debra A. Antonini, Laura L. Austin, Mary B. Campbell, Suzanne Nave Patrick, *Researchers*
Joan Hurst, *Editorial Assistant*
Artemis S. Lampathakis, *Illustrations Assistant*
Janet A. Dustin, *Art Secretary*
John D. Garst, Jr., Peter J. Balch, D. Mark Carlson, Joseph F. Ochlak, *Locator-map Research and Production*

STAFF FOR *FAR-OUT FUN!:* Patricia N. Holland, *Project Editor;* Catherine O'Neill, *Text Editor;* Louise Ponsford, *Designer;* Debra A. Antonini, Laura L. Austin, Suzanne Nave Patrick, *Researchers;* Sue Levin, *Artist*

ENGRAVING, PRINTING, AND PRODUCT MANUFACTURE
Robert W. Messer, *Manager;* George V. White, *Production Manager;* George J. Zeller, Jr., *Production Project Manager;* Mark R. Dunlevy, David V. Showers, Gregory Storer, *Assistant Production Managers;* Mary A. Bennett, *Production Assistant;* Julia F. Warner, *Production Staff Assistant*

STAFF ASSISTANTS: Nancy F. Berry, Elizabeth A. Brazerol, Dianne T. Craven, Carol R. Curtis, Lori E. Davie, Mary Elizabeth Davis, Ann Di Fiore, Rosamund Garner, Bernadette L. Grigonis, Annie Hampford, Virginia W. Hannasch, Nancy J. Harvey, Cleo Petroff, Nancy E. Simson, Pamela Black Townsend, Virginia A. Williams

MARKET RESEARCH: Mark W. Brown, Joseph S. Fowler, Carrla L. Holmes, Meg McElligott Kieffer, Nancy Serbin, Susan D. Snell, Barbara Steinwurtzel

INDEX: Teresa P. Barry